THE
ASTRONOMY
BOOK

by Jonathan F. Henry, Ph.D.

Master
Books

The Astronomy Book

First Printing: 1999
Fifth Printing: September 2006

Printed in China

Cover Design by Janell Robertson
Interior Design by Brent Spurlock and Janell Robertson

For information write:
Master Books
P.O. Box 726
Green Forest AR, 72638

Please visit our website for other great titles:
www.masterbooks.net

ISBN-13: 978-0-89051-250-0
ISBN-10: 0-89051-250-7

Library of Congress: 99-070077

Dedication

To Sharon,

and Faith, David, Daniel, and Charity

Contents

Introduction. The Wonder of Astronomy 5

Chapter 1. What Is Astronomy? 6
    What Do Astronomers Study? 7

Chapter 2. How Big Is the Universe? .8
    Some Cosmic Distances 8
    Will Astronomers Ever See the Edge of the Universe? 10
    Are There Other Universes? 10
    How Do Astronomers Know How Far Away the Stars Are? 11
    Solar System and Universe Facts 12

Chapter 3. The Origin of the Universe 14
    When Did God Make Moons and Planets? 15
    Is the Solar System in the Bible? 15
    Was There a Big Bang? 16
    The Importance of the Biblical Record 17
    Is the Universe Expanding? 17

Chapter 4. Watching the Sky 18
    Eclipses of the Sun 19
    Eclipses of the Moon 20
    Using a Telescope 20

Chapter 5. Why Did God Create the Heavenly Bodies? 22
    Calendars 23
    Modern Time-Telling 24
    What Are Constellations? 24
    How Are Constellations Related to Astrology? 25
    How Do Astronomers Use the Constellations? 26
    Learning More About the Constellations 27

Chapter 6. Space Exploration 28
    Early Rockets 28
    The Space Age 29
    The First Moon Landing 30
    The Modern Space Program 31
    Unmanned Missions 32
    What Has The Space Program Taught Us? 34
    Space Highlights 34

Chapter 7. A Tour of the Solar System 36
    The Earth: Not Just Another Planet .36
    Why Did God Make Other Planets? .37
    The Moon: A Special Satellite 38
    The Origin of the Moon 38
    How Old Is the Moon? 39
    The Sun, a Light-Giver 40
    The Sun: Not Just Another Star 40

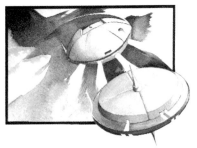

Where Does the Sun Get Its Heat? 42
How Old Is the Sun? 43
The Nebular Hypothesis: A False Idea 43
Mercury and Venus 44
Mars: Not a Life-Supporting Planet 45
Jupiter and Saturn 46
Uranus and Neptune 48
Pluto. 49

Chapter 8. Stars and Galaxies 50
What Are Stars Made Of? 51
Stars Are Not All the Same 52
Do Black Holes Exist? 53
The Closest Galaxies 54
Seeing Distant Objects in a Young Universe .55
Look-Back Time 55

Chapter 9. Cosmic Catastrophes 56
Star Death 56
The Death of the Sun 57
Supernova Remnants 57
The Myth of Star Birth 59

Chapter 10. Catastrophes in the Solar System 60
Did Moons Really Explode? 61
What Are Asteroids? Where Did They Come From? 62
Did a Planet Really Explode? 62
Martian Catastrophes 64
The Martian Flood 65
What Caused These Catastrophes? When Were They? 66
Comets 67
The Age of Comets 68
Meteor Showers 68
Big Meteor Craters 69
Did an Asteroid or Meteor Kill the Dinosaurs? 70
Big Meteorites 70
People Have Seen Big Meteors Land 71

Chapter 11. Are There Other Planets in Other Solar Systems? .72
Why Do Some Astronomers Believe There Are Other Solar Systems? .73
Is There Extraterrestrial Life? 74
What Is Life? 74
What Are UFOs? 75

Endnotes and Credits 76
Glossary 77
Index 78

Introduction:
The Wonder of Astronomy

Who has not looked into the heavens on a starry night with a sense of wonder? We see in the night sky the vastness of the universe. We have the feeling that some awesome power is responsible for it. Did you know that God designed us to respond this way?

The Bible in Psalm 19:1 tells us that "the heavens declare the glory of God." God made us in His image so we are able to sense His handiwork in the heavens. This makes astronomy one of the most fascinating sciences. It is also one of the most misunderstood sciences. As we will see, it has been twisted into corrupted forms more than perhaps any other science. Millions of people trust in the satanic perversion of astronomy called "astrology," or the atheistic perversion of astronomy called "cosmic evolution."

Astronomy is not astrology, nor is it cosmic evolution. Genuine astronomy is one of the most beautiful sciences because it shows us the glory of God in His creation.

Chapter 1

WHAT IS ASTRONOMY?

A stronomy is the branch of science dealing with the sun, the moon, the planets, and the stars. The word "astronomy" comes from two Greek words meaning "knowledge of the stars." An astronomer is a person who has scientific knowledge about the stars and other heavenly bodies.

Astronomy should not be confused with astrology. Astrology is a false science which comes from ancient paganism. It is the belief that the stars can predict our future and set the course for our lives. The Bible teaches that only God can guide our lives, a truth repeated again and again in verses like Psalm 143:8 and James 4:13–15.

A view of the earth and moon as seen from outer space.

What Do Astronomers Study?

The sun

The moon

The nine planets

Stars and galaxies of the universe.

Astronomers study the sun, the moon, and the planets and their moons, all of which are considered to make up the solar system. What is the difference between moons and planets? We picture planets orbiting the Sun, and moons orbit planets.

Astronomers also study stars outside the solar system. Stars produce their own light, but planets shine by reflected light. All the objects in the heavens are called "celestial bodies."

The only star in the solar system is the sun. The sun's gravitation holds nine known planets. There may possibly be undiscovered planets beyond the ones we know. Most of the planets have one or more moons which orbit them. The earth has one moon, and at the other extreme some planets have many known moons. Mercury and Venus have no moon.

Aside from the sun, all other stars are far outside the solar system. They are in groups called galaxies, and the galaxies themselves are in larger groups called "galaxy clusters."

Astronomers estimate that the portion of the universe we can see has about 100 billion galaxies, each with an average of about 100 billion stars. The solar system itself is located in the Milky Way Galaxy which has somewhere between 200 and 300 billion stars.

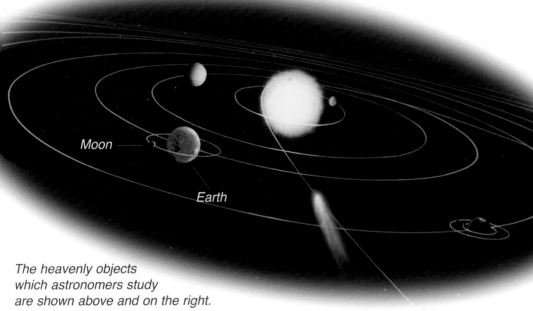

Moon

Earth

The heavenly objects which astronomers study are shown above and on the right.

7

Chapter 2

HOW BIG IS THE UNIVERSE?

The size of the universe has never been measured. The solar system itself is so large that it staggers the imagination. The moon, the closest celestial body to us, is nearly 250,000 miles away. To travel this far, you would have to circle the earth ten times.

The nearest planet is Venus. The distance of Venus varies but sometimes is as close as 24 million miles. The sun is nearly 100 million miles away. This is so far that a beam of light traveling 186,000 miles per second needs eight minutes for the trip.

This illustration of the solar system shows all nine planets, the asteroid belt, and the sun. The planets, beginning at the sun, are Mercury, Venus, Earth, Mars, Jupiter, Saturn, Uranus, Neptune, and Pluto.

Some Cosmic Distances

- **Closest Celestial Object to Earth:** the moon, 239,000 miles

- **Closest Planet to Earth:** Venus, 24 million miles at closest approach

- **Closest Star Outside the Solar System:** Proxima Centauri, 4 ½ light-years

- **Closest Independent Galaxy Outside the Milky Way:** Andromeda, about 2 million light-years

Outside the solar system, the closest star is Proxima Centauri, very near Alpha Centauri. It is about 25 trillion miles away. This is so far that a beam of light traveling 186,000 miles per second requires 4 ½ years to make the trip. In other words, light from Alpha Centauri takes 4 ½ years to get to us.

Such distances are so huge that astronomers have made a special way to talk about them. Light travels 186,000 miles per second, which is 6 trillion miles per year. The distance light travels in one year is called a "light-year," and is 6 trillion miles. We can say that Alpha Centauri is 25 trillion miles away, or 4 ½ light-years away. Remember, the light-year measures distance, not time.

The independent galaxy nearest the Milky Way is the Andromeda Galaxy. It is about 2 million light-years away. At this distance, light traveling at 186,000 miles per second would take 2 million years to reach us.

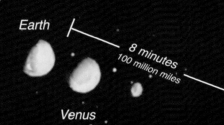

Earth

8 minutes
100 million miles

Venus

Light travels at
186,000 *MILES PER SECOND!*

- It takes 8 minutes for light to travel from the sun to the earth.

- It takes 4 ½ *YEARS* for light to travel from the sun to the closest star, Proxima Centauri.

Will Astronomers Ever See the Edge of the Universe?

Astronomers believe that certain objects called quasars are the farthest they have seen. Most astronomers think that quasars are about 14 billion light-years away. However, the universe extends farther than any astronomer can see, even with the most powerful telescopes.

Never has any telescope seen the "edge" of the universe. More powerful telescopes simply reveal more galaxies which astronomers have never seen before.

Radio telescopes listen to signals traveling from deep in space to "see" objects such as quasars. As astronomers build larger telescopes to see further into space, they only reveal more wonders of God's creation.

Jeremiah, the Old Testament prophet, prophesied that man would never completely explore all of the universe.

Are There Other Universes?

Scientists have observed no other universes. By definition, the universe includes the entire physical creation. If we could observe another universe, it would actually be a part of this one.

The Old Testament prophet Jeremiah, mindful of the infinite reach of God's power, realized that man would never probe the heavens completely. Jeremiah 31:37 states that if man could completely probe the heavens, God would cast Israel off.

Since God will never abandon Israel, astronomers will never see the "edge" of the stars. Astronomers will never completely probe even this one universe.

How Do Astronomers Know How Far Away the Stars Are?

When you are traveling down a country road, the trees and buildings next to the roadside seem to move past you much faster than the trees and mountains in the distance. The speed at which

View of three stars

Very far away (not moved)

Far away (moved a little)

Close (moved a lot)

View of same three stars several months later

objects appear to move past you depends on how close or far they are. Very distant objects do not seem to move at all.

Astronomers have a name for this situation. It is called "parallax." A nearby object has high parallax, and a faraway object has low parallax.

Imagine the earth orbiting the sun. Since the earth is nearly 100 million miles from the sun, the orbit would be almost 200 million miles across. Astronomers on the earth can see nearby stars, such as Alpha Centauri, moving against a background of distant stars that do not seem to move

at all. The nearby stars have high parallax, and the distant stars have low parallax.

Even the closest stars are so far away that the parallax for them is very small. Astronomers cannot observe the parallax of even the closest stars without powerful telescopes. Even so, astronomers have been able to measure the parallax for many stars. Once the parallax for a star is known, there is a certain mathematical equation which allows for calculation of the distance to the star.

If a star is too far away, even the most powerful telescopes cannot detect any parallax. The maximum distance for detecting parallax is about 600 light-years from the earth.

How do astronomers estimate distances for stars farther than 600 light-years? The methods are indirect and are quite uncertain. For instance, most astronomers estimate that the most distant objects, the quasars, are 14 billion light-years away, but some astronomers think this distance is too small. Other astronomers think this distance may be as much as 100 times too large. If this were true, the quasars could be as close as 140 million light-years.

Regardless of uncertainties in cosmic distances, however, the universe is extremely vast and is a powerful testimony to the all-powerful might of the Creator.

If you are looking out the window in a moving car, the objects close to you (trees and house) are moving fast while the mountains in the distance don't seem to move at all. Astronomers use this same idea (parallax) to measure the distance to the stars by observing how fast the stars are moving compared to each other (above).

Solar System and Universe Facts

Universe Facts

Jupiter's moon, Io (left), has the MOST VIOLENT volcanic eruptions known anywhere in the solar system.

Number of Galaxies: estimated at 100 billion in the observable universe

Average Number of Stars Per Galaxy: estimated at 100 billion

Farthest Objects Seen to Date: quasars (as much as 20 billion light-years away)

Size of the Observable Universe: very uncertain; 20 billion light-years maximum; may be as low as 7 billion light-years

Total Size of the Entire Universe: unknown

Earth

Sun

This illustration shows what the solar system might look like if you were on Pluto. In a real photo, the Sun and planets would be so small as to be nearly invisible.

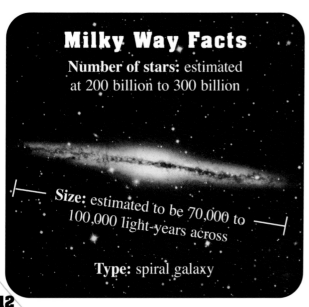

Milky Way Facts

Number of stars: estimated at 200 billion to 300 billion

Size: estimated to be 70,000 to 100,000 light-years across

Type: spiral galaxy

Planet Facts

Closest to the sun: Mercury

Farthest from the sun: Pluto

Hottest surface: Venus (900°F, 500°C)

Coldest surface: Pluto (-400°F, -250°C)

Biggest planet: Jupiter (1,000 times larger than earth*)

Smallest planet: Pluto (200 times smaller than earth*)

Longest day: Venus (rotates once every 243 earth days)

Shortest day: Jupiter (rotates once every 10 hours)

Longest year: Pluto (248 earth years)

Shortest year: Mercury (88 earth days)

* Comparison by volume

Order of the Planets (going out from the sun)
Mercury, Venus, Earth, Mars, Jupiter,
Saturn, Uranus, Neptune, Pluto

Sun Facts

Size: nearly 1 million miles across

Relative size: 1,000 times larger than Jupiter*, 1 million times larger than earth*

Surface temperature: about 10,000°F (6,000°C)

Temperature at center: unknown; may be millions of degrees

Average distance from earth: 93 million miles

Jupiter (below) is 1,000 times LARGER than Earth, but rotates so FAST that one full day on Jupiter lasts only 10 hours.

Did You Know?

1. Mars (lower left) is nicknamed "the Red Planet." It looks red because it has lots of iron oxide, better known as rust.

2. Jupiter's moon, Io, is rich in sulfur. It has the most violent volcanic eruptions known anywhere in the solar system.

3. Saturn weighs only seven-tenths as much as an equal volume of water. If there were a bathtub big enough to hold Saturn, it would float.

4. Methane (natural gas) freezes at -259°F (-184°C), but Pluto is so cold that it has "snowstorms" of solid methane crystals.

5. If the earth were as cold as Pluto, nearly all the gases in our atmosphere would be frozen solid.

Mars is called the Red Planet because it contains large amounts of rust.

Saturn weighs only seven-tenths as much as an equal volume of water. If there were a bathtub big enough to hold Saturn, it would float.

Chapter 3

THE ORIGIN OF THE UNIVERSE

Many scientists claim that the universe developed on its own by a process called cosmic evolution. Some scientists who believe in cosmic evolution also claim that God used this process to make the universe. Some of these scientists and other Christian leaders have even called this process of cosmic evolution the "creation" of the universe.

However, "creation" by cosmic evolution is not true biblical creation at all. The Bible in Genesis 1:1 states, "In the beginning God created the heaven and the earth." The word "created" in Genesis 1:1 is the translation of a Hebrew word which means "creation out of nothing." The creation of the universe was a supernatural act. It was an event of creation, not a process of evolution.

A big problem with cosmic evolution is that there has not been enough time for it. Cosmic evolution would require a very long time, so some scientists claim that the universe is anywhere from 7 billion to 20 billion years old. Scientific data do not support these estimates. In fact, many types of scientific evidence indicate that the universe is only a few thousand years old.

One of the biggest problems for those believing in cosmic evolution is explaining where all the structure in the universe came from. How could stars form and then organize themselves into galaxies, and how could the galaxies form clusters of galaxies? Scientists who believe in evolution have no answer to this question, because no one has ever seen stars (or anything else) arising out of nothing.

The Word of God, however, does answer this question. The Bible says that God created and organized the universe by His infinitely powerful spoken word. Psalm 33:6 tells us, "By the word of the Lord were the heavens made."

The Milky Way Galaxy is made up of billions of stars including our own sun. The universe is so perfectly organized that it could not happen by chance. It must have been created by God.

When Did God Make Moons and Planets?

At first glance, Genesis chapter 1 does not seem to mention moons and planets. However, Genesis 1:16 tells us that God "made the stars."

To ancient peoples, the word "stars" included every celestial object besides the sun and the moon. The Hebrew word for "stars" in Genesis 1:16 therefore includes the creation of the planets and their moons. This broad meaning of the word "stars" continued until only a couple of centuries ago.

Ancient peoples knew the planets Mercury, Venus, Mars, Jupiter, and Saturn. They may also have known of Uranus and Neptune, as well as some of the large moons of Jupiter. Ancient believers in the true God of creation knew that He had created these heavenly bodies.

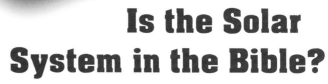

Saturn and its rings

Is the Solar System in the Bible?

The Bible does not mention the solar system. The concept of the solar system is a man-made idea.

Though we often picture the planets orbiting the sun, we would see no orbits in space if we could see the sun and all the planets from very far away.

Furthermore, God's view of the sun and all the planets is focused on the earth.

Of all the planets, the earth is the only one to which God sent His Son, and the earth is the only planet to which Christ will come a second time.

The ancients did not have the concept of a solar system. This did not prevent them from making the types of celestial predictions astronomers make today. Ancient peoples predicted solar eclipses, lunar eclipses, and planetary appearances, as well as the coming of the new year, seasons, months, and days, just as modern astronomers do.

People have been studying the stars for thousands of years. Galileo used his early telescope to observe the heavens.

Was There a Big Bang?

Believers in cosmic evolution say that a hypothetical (imaginary) event called the "big bang" started the universe. The big bang is supposed to be a cosmic explosion which happened billions of years ago. The explosion supposedly blasted matter out through space which slowly condensed into all the planets and stars we see today.

The big bang would have been the biggest explosion ever. But when has an explosion led to more order and structure than there was before? Such a thing has never been observed. Since science has never observed it, the big bang is only a belief, not science.

The best evidence that the big bang never happened (apart from biblical statements) is the intricate structure and organization of the universe, with stars grouped into galaxies and galaxies grouped into clusters. Unfortunately, some scientists refer to the big bang as "the moment of creation," even though the big bang is the opposite of biblical creation.

According to the Bible, the Creator made the universe perfect. Genesis 1:31 says that "God saw everything that He had made, and, behold, it was very good." Biblical creation and the big bang are exact opposites and cannot be reconciled. There was never a big bang.

The Importance of the Biblical Record

Today no one can observe an act of creation anywhere. The Bible teaches that the creation is finished (Gen. 2:1). No one can see cosmic evolution either, though some scientists say they can. When a scientist claims to have seen cosmic evolution, we need to ask what has the scientist really observed?

Astronomers, for example, have observed clouds of gas surrounding certain stars. Some scientists reach the conclusion that this means stars are evolving, because they believe in the evolution of stars from gas clouds. However, no one has observed any evolution. The real observation is the gas clouds. The evolution of stars is supposed to take millions, if not billions, of years. Obviously, no one, not even a succession of observers over many thousands of years, could ever hope to see the evolution of a star.

Since no one can observe either creation or cosmic evolution, we must be willing to accept the Word of the Creator about the beginning of the universe. However, we are not forced to have a blind faith in creation. God has made the universe to reveal himself and His power (Rom. 1:20), including His creative power. As we will see, there are many astronomical evidences which confirm that God created the universe.

Is the Universe Expanding?

According to the idea of the big bang, the universe began expanding at the moment of the big bang explosion and has been expanding ever since. The idea of an expanding universe and the belief in the big bang are related.

Since there never was a big bang, it is an open question whether the universe is expanding. There is some evidence that there might not be any universal expansion at all.

Astronomers who believe that the universe is expanding point to a phenomenon called the "red shift" as proof that they are right. Other astronomers say that the red shift can be explained by causes having nothing to do with the big bang. Thus, there is no proof that the universe is expanding.

"God saw everything that He had made, and, behold, it was very good" (Gen. 1:31).

Chapter 4

WATCHING THE SKY

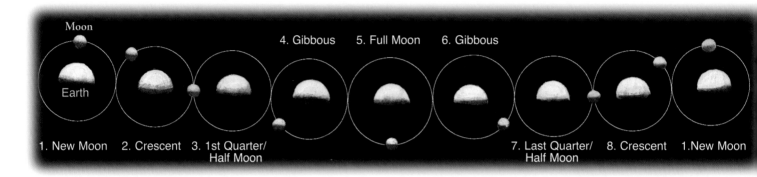

Moon

Earth

4. Gibbous   5. Full Moon   6. Gibbous

1. New Moon   2. Crescent   3. 1st Quarter/   7. Last Quarter/   8. Crescent   1.New Moon
Half Moon   Half Moon

It is easy to begin sky-watching because you need only your eyes to get started. On most cloudless nights the moon is the brightest object in the sky. You can begin your study of astronomy by observing the phases of the moon, or "lunar phases."

The moon takes about one month to orbit the earth, or more precisely, 29 1/2 days. During this time the moon goes through four phases, each visible for about one week. In each phase the moon has a different appearance. The first phase is "new moon" in which the moon is not visible at all. In this phase, the moon is between the earth and the sun, and we on earth are facing the dark side of the moon which we cannot see against the night sky.

As the moon passes from the first phase to the second phase, it becomes larger and more visible night by night. After about a week it looks like a half-circle. This is the "first quarter moon."

The visible part of the moon continues to grow, and a week later the moon is in its third phase, or "full moon." This is when the moon is on the side of the earth opposite the sun, and the moon is fully illuminated. It looks like a circle.

After another week comes the fourth phase, the "last quarter moon." The moon looks like a semicircle as in first quarter phase. After last quarter phase the visible part of the moon shrinks to enter "new moon" and begin the cycle of phases over again.

For added enjoyment in watching the lunar phases, you may want to obtain a pair of binoculars. Binoculars make the moon look two to five times larger than normal, depending on the power of the lenses. In a magnified lunar image, it is easy to spot beautiful craters such as the large crater Copernicus. There are lunar maps for identifying features on the surface of the moon. *National Geographic* has published excellent lunar maps through the years.

Eclipses of the Sun

One of the most exciting experiences for all people, professional astronomers and lay people alike, is the opportunity to see eclipses of the sun and the moon.

Solar eclipses occur when the moon passes between the sun and the earth. Anyone on the earth inside the resulting shadow of the moon will experience a total solar eclipse. The sun itself looks black, and is surrounded by a shining halo of solar gases called the "corona," which is not normally visible. On the earth, darkness descends and birds may begin to roost as they would at night.

Total eclipses are very rare and last only a few minutes, so a person is very fortunate to see even one during his lifetime. At a particular location, a total eclipse can be expected only once every few centuries.

Partial eclipses of the sun are much more common. During a partial eclipse, the moon does not completely cover the sun. On the earth one sees the landscape illuminated in a strange kind of half-light coming from the partly covered sun high in the sky, unlike the normal twilight of sunset.

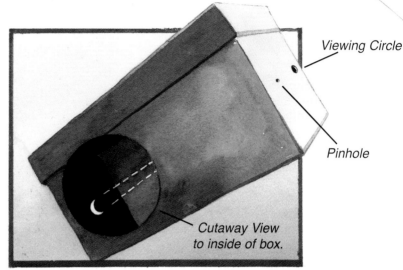

Viewing Circle

Pinhole

Cutaway View to inside of box.

During a solar eclipse, a person can experience permanent eye damage by looking directly at the sun. The eclipse can be viewed safely by making a pin-hole camera with a shoe-box.

At a given location, partial eclipses happen as often as every 10 or 15 years.

Never look at the sun directly, even during a partial eclipse. The sun is thousands of times brighter than our eyes can stand, and even during a partial eclipse the sun is dangerous to look at. To view a solar eclipse, you can make a "pinhole camera." To make your pinhole camera, paint the inside length of a shoe box black. (Your camera will work satisfactorily even if the shoe box is not painted inside.)

Make a tiny pinhole in one end of the shoe box. A couple of inches from the pinhole, cut a small viewing circle about the size of a pencil. Put the cover on the shoe box and aim the pinhole at the eclipse. Through the viewing circle you can observe the sun's image on the inside of the shoe box at the other end. It will look white and the eclipsed portion will be dark. You may also see the dark spots called "sunspots" that are sometimes on the sun's surface.

A solar eclipse is caused by the moon passing between the earth and the sun, blocking out the sun's light. During a total eclipse, the shining halo of solar gases called the "corona" is visible around the edges of the sun.

Eclipses of the Moon

Lunar eclipses happen when the earth is between the sun and the moon, in other words, when the moon is in full phase. A lunar eclipse does not happen at every full moon. At a given locality, lunar eclipses happen every few years. Not only are lunar eclipses fairly common, they are also safe to look at directly.

When the moon is fully eclipsed it shines a dull red. Although there is no

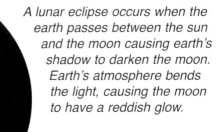

A lunar eclipse occurs when the earth passes between the sun and the moon causing earth's shadow to darken the moon. Earth's atmosphere bends the light, causing the moon to have a reddish glow.

sunlight falling directly on it, the earth's atmosphere bends some sunlight around the earth, especially the red colors like those we see at sunset.

In a partial lunar eclipse, the earth partly covers the moon, making a circular shadow which is obvious to observers on earth. This shows that the earth is round, a fact known to the ancient Hebrews. It was common knowledge in biblical times that the earth is a sphere, as mentioned in Isaiah 40:22 which refers to the "circle" or roundness of the earth. Even Columbus knew the earth is round, a fact now acknowledged by many modern historians.[1]

The diagram at the left shows the difference between a solar and a lunar eclipse.

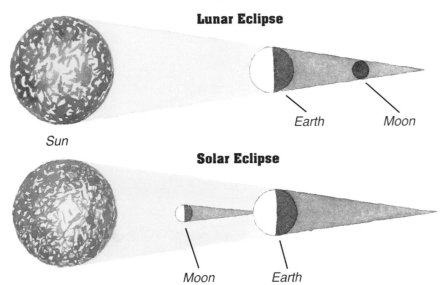

Lunar Eclipse

Sun

Earth   Moon

Solar Eclipse

Moon   Earth

Using a Telescope

Telescopes for amateur astronomers are of two types, the refracting type and the reflecting type. These two types are often called simply the "refractor" and the "reflector." The refractor has been in use since Galileo's time. Today most astronomers prefer the reflecting telescope, the type first perfected by Isaac Newton.

Sometimes called the "Newtonian reflector," the reflecting telescope has a design per-

mitting more magnifying power in less space than the refracting type. Most telescopes used by professional astronomers are reflectors. The Hubble Space Telescope, launched into the earth orbit in 1990 by the United States at a cost of billions of dollars, is a very sophisticated reflector.

Good reflecting telescopes are available at department stores starting at about $300, or you can order one from a scientific supply

The space shuttle is using its robotic arm to lift the Hubble telescope out of the shuttle cargo bay.

house such as Fisher Scientific or Edmund Scientific.

When you buy a reflector, look for a power of less than 100 times (100 X) or so, and also be sure to buy one with an opening for light, or "aperture," that is several inches wide. Many cheap telescopes advertise a high power but have a small aperture, which means that little light gets onto the magnifying lenses, and the image, though magnified, will be dim.

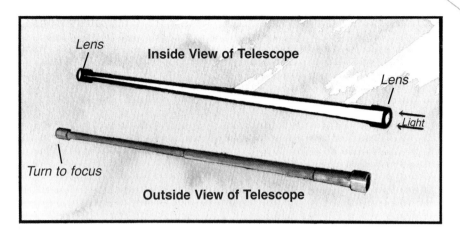

An early telescope was made simply by placing two lenses in a hollow tube. The smaller lens could be adjusted in and out of the tube to focus the view of the telescope.

Amateur telescopic viewing is most enjoyable with the planets, since stars do not look much different through an amateur's telescope than they do to the unaided eye. You can see features you could never see otherwise — the markings and polar caps of Mars (once thought to be the abode of alien civilizations), the Great Red Spot of Jupiter (a centuries-old storm), and Saturn's rings (an exploded moon or moons).

Every month, the magazine *Sky and Telescope* publishes tables and charts showing which planets are visible and where they will be. *Sky and Telescope* is available in most libraries, and a yearly subscription is relatively inexpensive. *The World Almanac* for each year publishes similar information in a briefer form.

Chapter 5

WHY DID GOD CREATE THE HEAVENLY BODIES?

Science can suggest some answers to this question. Biologists have found that many species of birds and insects are guided in their migrations by patterns of stars in the sky. The star patterns are like a map to help them navigate.

God created the stars on day four of the creation week, as recorded in Genesis 1:16, before He created the flying creatures (including birds) on day five, and the creeping things (including insects) on day six. God created the stars first to ensure that these creatures would be able to navigate to find food.

Many birds and insects migrate thousands of miles a year. The monarch butterfly makes a 3,000-mile round trip. Biologists believe that they might use the sun, the closest star, to help find their way.

Star patterns, as well as the positions of the sun, moon, and planets, are used in human navigation as well. Without special training, you can use the sun's position in the sky to find the direction in which you are traveling. For example, if the sun is in the west, and you are traveling away from the sun, you know that you are going east.

God provided a way for people and animals to find their way using the stars long before the compass was invented.

The most complex navigational systems of all, the inertial guidance systems used for commercial air flight and interplanetary space travel, also sight the positions of the sun and stars to stay on course. The remarkable Voyager 2 space probe discussed in the next chapter stayed on course in its journey through the solar system by star tracking.

As to the ultimate purpose of the heavenly bodies, science can give no answers. Some people speculate that God made them to support other "solar systems," perhaps with planets harboring other forms of life. However, we can learn the true answers to questions about purpose only by accepting the revelation of the Creator. Only the Creator knows why He made the heavenly bodies, and only in the Bible does the Creator tell us why He made them.

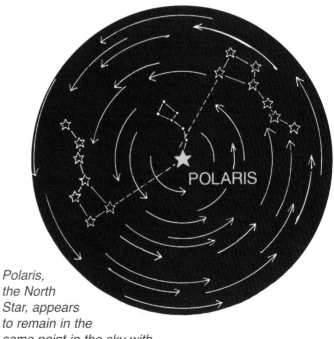

Polaris, the North Star, appears to remain in the same point in the sky with the other stars rotating around it. You can always find the North Star by following the line from the two end stars of the Big Dipper.

POLARIS

In Genesis 1:14–18 we read that God created the sun and the moon to give light upon the earth.

In addition, the sun, the moon, and also the stars (including planets) were created to mark off seasons, days, and years. In other words, God made the celestial bodies as time-tellers to measure intervals of time.

Ancient peoples generally knew how to tell the time of day or night within the equivalent of half an hour or so, simply by noting the position of sun or stars in the sky. Ancient peoples also routinely measured the passage of seasons and years in this way.

People began telling time simply by noting the position of the sun in the sky. Later, inventions such as the sundial were more accurate but were still based on God's creation.

Calendars

Quarter　　*Full Moon*　　*Quarter*

The moon has always been used for time-telling. It is the basis for the so-called "lunar calendar" in which the passing of each month is marked by the changing position of the moon in the sky. The word "month" in fact comes from the word "moon."

A lunar month begins on the night when the first phase (new moon) begins to show the first thin crescent of light. Of all the lunar phase changes, this one is the easiest to see. New moon is, therefore, the first phase of the new month, which is why this phase is called "new moon." The passing of each lunar month is easy to follow by watching the sequence of lunar phases.

The ease of knowing when a lunar month begins and ends has made the lunar calendar very popular throughout history. The Hebrew

The phases of the moon start when the moon is completely invisible. It then slowly grows larger until the entire moon is lit up in the full phase. Then it slowly gets thinner until it is back to a new moon, where the cycle begins over again. In the northern hemisphere the lunar phases move across the sky from right to left. In the southern hemisphere the phases move from left to right. The lunar calender is based on these lunar phases.

calendar used in the Bible was a lunar calendar. To this day the official calendar of Israel and the Arab nations is a lunar one.

The calendar used in many countries today is the "solar calendar," based on the "solar year." The solar year is officially defined as the time required for the sun to return to the sky position of the previous January 1. We can think of the solar year as the time the earth takes to go around the sun once.

Modern Time-Telling

Modern civilization continues to use the celestial bodies to tell time. All clocks on earth are synchronized with Greenwich Mean Time (GMT), also called universal time or "Zulu" time. Greenwich (pronounced "GRIN-itch") is a suburb of London, England.

Every day at Greenwich, astronomers note the position of the sun, a daily procedure which is nearly 200 years old. When the sun passes directly overhead, as observed through a special solar telescope, it is said to be exactly noon GMT. All clocks on earth are set by GMT.

Clocks in a time zone east or west of Greenwich are set to show a different hour than at Greenwich, but the hours begin and end at the same moment nearly everywhere on the globe. In the eastern time zone of the United States, the sun is directly overhead five hours after it is noon in the Greenwich time zone. When it is noon in Greenwich, it is only 7 a.m. in the eastern time zone. When it is 12 noon in the eastern time zone, it is 5 p.m. in Greenwich.

It is easy to see that modern civilization relies on the sun, moon, and stars for exactly the same reasons given in Genesis 1:14–18.

Furthermore, all the known purposes of the heavenly bodies, both the purposes revealed in Scripture and the functions suggested by science, are for the benefit of life on earth. This shows that the earth and life on the earth are very special in God's sight. The earth is the focus of the Creator's attention.

All clocks are set with Greenwich Mean Time (GMT) with a transit telescope similar to the telescope above. It precisely measures when the sun is directly overhead.

What Are Constellations?

The constellations are certain star patterns which historians say have been recognized by many cultures since around 2500 B.C. This date is approximately the time of the dispersion from the Tower of Babel, described in Genesis chapters 10 and 11.

Since most cultures recognize more or less the same constellations, it is evident that all peoples

Constellations are groups of stars that have an imaginary picture associated with them. The constellation Ursa Major (the bear) shown above also includes the well-known shape of the Big Dipper.

used to live at one place and have spread from there. The Bible in Genesis identifies this place as Babel.

There is no other known reason that different peoples at different times would perceive the same star patterns among the thousands of stars in the sky. Orion, "the Hunter," for instance, is a constellation recognized under a variety of names by almost all cultures.

What would cause most of the world's cultures to imagine a hunter in the sky (Orion), or a bear (Ursa Major), or a serpent (Serpens)? The answer seems to be that the constellations were known at Babel when all peoples were united. They carried their memories of these sky pictures with them when they left Babel.

The star chart above is a navigational chart that sailors in the 19ᵗʰ century used for navigation. The basic patterns of the constellations are shared by many cultures around the world.

How Are Constellations Related to Astrology?

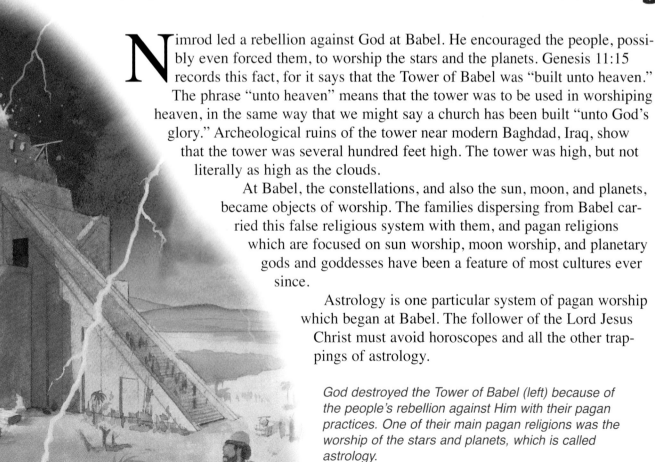

Nimrod led a rebellion against God at Babel. He encouraged the people, possibly even forced them, to worship the stars and the planets. Genesis 11:15 records this fact, for it says that the Tower of Babel was "built unto heaven." The phrase "unto heaven" means that the tower was to be used in worshiping heaven, in the same way that we might say a church has been built "unto God's glory." Archeological ruins of the tower near modern Baghdad, Iraq, show that the tower was several hundred feet high. The tower was high, but not literally as high as the clouds.

At Babel, the constellations, and also the sun, moon, and planets, became objects of worship. The families dispersing from Babel carried this false religious system with them, and pagan religions which are focused on sun worship, moon worship, and planetary gods and goddesses have been a feature of most cultures ever since.

Astrology is one particular system of pagan worship which began at Babel. The follower of the Lord Jesus Christ must avoid horoscopes and all the other trappings of astrology.

God destroyed the Tower of Babel (left) because of the people's rebellion against Him with their pagan practices. One of their main pagan religions was the worship of the stars and planets, which is called astrology.

How Do Astronomers Use the Constellations?

Astronomers have defined 88 constellations spanning the entire sky. In this total are the original ancient constellations, plus a number of new ones which have been devised in the past several centuries. There are also some familiar star groups which are not defined as constellations, such as the Big Dipper and the Little Dipper. These are called "asterisms."

The 88 astronomical constellations are used in mapping the sky. Like states on a map of the United States, each astronomical constellation covers an exact area of the sky with distinct boundaries.

portion of the sky centered around the constellation Andromeda.

Astronomers use a system of star names based on the constellations. The brightest star in a constellation is usually given the Greek letter

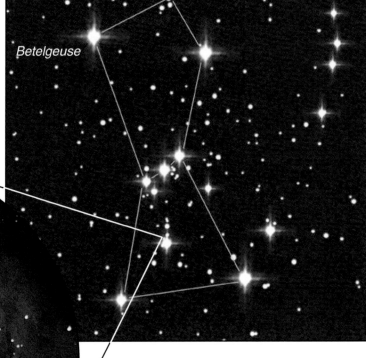

Betelgeuse

Astronomers use the constellations as a reference to find other celestial objects. By finding the constellation of Orion (above), one can easily find the Orion Nebula (left) with a good telescope. Some of the brightest stars also have common names. A prominent star in Orion is Alpha-Orionis, but is often called Betelgeuse.

Astronomers can designate the location of any celestial object by simply noting the constellation it is in, just as we would talk about the location of a city by specifying the state where it is. The Andromeda Galaxy, for instance, is officially called the Great Galaxy in Andromeda, because it appears in the

alpha, followed by the name (slightly modified) of the constellation it is in. Alpha Centauri, for instance, is the brightest star in the constellation Centaur. The next brightest star is designated beta, and so on down the Greek alphabet.

There are several other naming systems not based on the constellations. Two common ones are the Messier system and the NGC system. These are based on two famous catalogs of celestial objects. The Messier catalog was developed by a French astronomer, and the New General Catalog (NGC) is published by

Cambridge University and is periodically updated to include new discoveries.

In these catalog-based systems, the name of a celestial object is the catalog name (Messier or NGC) followed by the number of the catalog entry. The Andromeda Galaxy is the 31st entry in the Messier catalog, so it is Messier 31 or simply M 31. The Andromeda Galaxy is also listed in the New General Catalog as entry 224, so it is NGC 224.

Learning More About the Constellations

The Astronomical Society of the Pacific has published excellent constellation and star guides in booklet form and on audio cassette. With these inexpensive resources, you can learn the constellations by watching the sky during any season of the year. These materials are in some public libraries, or you may write to the following:

Astronomical Society of the Pacific, 390 Ashton Avenue, San Francisco, CA 94112.

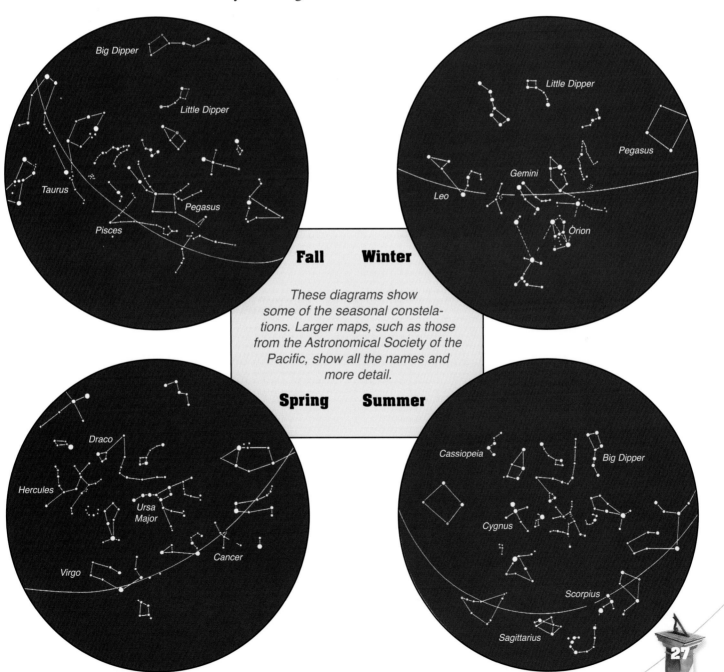

These diagrams show some of the seasonal constellations. Larger maps, such as those from the Astronomical Society of the Pacific, show all the names and more detail.

Chapter 6

SPACE EXPLORATION

W here were you on July 20, 1969? If you are a parent or an older adult, you may remember watching the first live telecast of astronauts landing on the moon. This was the climax of many years of rocket research.

Man has probably always dreamed of traveling to worlds in outer space. Though the Chinese experimented with rockets many centuries ago, most of their rocketry was for military use. It was not until the 19th century that space travel seemed technologically feasible. The French science fiction writer Jules Verne captured the public imagination with stories made into movies such as the 1902 silent film *A Trip to the Moon*.

With the development of new chemical fuels in the late 1800s, it was only a matter of time until practical rockets would be built. The big hurdle in designing rockets for space travel was to find a way for a rocket ship to carry its own oxygen. Unlike airplane or jet travel in the earth's atmosphere, where oxygen is available for burning fuel, rocket travel in the vacuum of space requires carrying not only rocket fuel, but oxygen to burn the fuel.

Earthrise over the moon with the lunar module on the Apollo 15 mission.

Early Rockets

I n the 1920s and 1930s, the American scientist Robert H. Goddard built the first workable rockets. During World War II the Nazis feverishly worked on rockets as weapons to wreak havoc on the Allies. Using technology based on Goddard's work reported in public sources, Hitler sought to develop weapons of mass destruction which would bring England and the other Allies to their knees.

Working for Hitler's rocket-weapons program was a certain young man named Wernher von Braun. By the end of World War II, von Braun and his colleagues had built two kinds of rockets — the V-1 and the V-2 ("V" for "vengeance"), which were used to deliver explosive warheads against England.

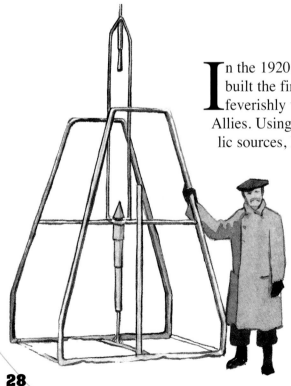

American scientist Robert H. Goddard is standing beside one of his first successful rockets. His pioneering experiments paved the way for the powerful Saturn V rocket that would place the first men on the moon.

The Space Age

The launch of the Sputnik satellite by the Russians in 1957 sparked the interest of the world and started the United States on its race to send the first man to the moon.

After World War II, Dr. von Braun and other German scientists came to the United States. Dr. von Braun assisted U.S. efforts to design military rockets in the early 1950s. Then came the Soviet launch of the satellite Sputnik (Russian for "satellite") into orbit on October 4, 1957.

In 1957 the Cold War was on, and Soviet claims of Sputnik's success were seen as a threat to American leadership of the free world. President Eisenhower called for a new emphasis on rocket research for peaceful purposes. As a result, the National Aeronautics and Space Administration (NASA) was launched on its career in 1958 under Dr. von Braun's scientific leadership.

In 1962, John Glenn became the first American to orbit the earth. He completed three orbits in his Freedom 7 capsule launched from Cape Canaveral. In the mid-1960s the massive Saturn V rocket engine with 7.5 million pounds of thrust was tested. This would be the engine which would blast the first lunar astronauts on their historic journey.

In preparation for the first moon landing, however, several missions were made to survey the lunar surface for a safe landing site free of boulders and craters. One such mission was the flight of the Apollo 8 spacecraft which approached the moon without landing on December 24, 1968. Dr. von Braun, chief scientific advisor of the entire multi-billion dollar moon-exploration program at NASA, by this time had become a Christian.

Under von Braun's influence, references to creation and the Bible were becoming increasingly evident at NASA. As the astronauts approached the moon that Christmas Eve in 1968, one of them began to read over a worldwide television hookup, "In the beginning God created the heaven and the earth. . . ."

Lt. Col. John H. Glenn became the first American to orbit the earth, in 1962. This Aurora 7 spacecraft and Atlas booster rocket was similar to the Freedom 7 used by Glenn in his historic flight.

The First Moon Landing

The first capsule to land on the moon, the Apollo 11 capsule, was launched from Cape Canaveral on July 16, 1969. Three astronauts were on their way to the moon. One of them, Michael Collins, would circle the moon in a lunar orbiter of the same design as the Apollo 8 capsule.

The other two astronauts, Neil Armstrong and Edwin Aldrin, would descend to the lunar surface in a smaller lunar landing module. On July 20, 1969, astronaut Armstrong became the first person ever to step on the moon's surface. He made the now historic declaration, "That's one small step for man, one giant leap for mankind."

The next day, after walking, jumping, and collecting moon rocks on the lunar surface, Armstrong and Aldrin lifted off from the

Man's first step on the moon was on July 20, 1969, by Neil Armstrong. His footprint (left) will last for centuries on the moon's airless surface.

There have been several missions to the moon since the Apollo 11 flight. Alan Shepard is shown below holding an American flag on the moon during the Apollo 14 mission.

moon using the small rocket engines in the landing module. The two astronauts were reunited with Collins in the lunar orbiter a few minutes later. All three arrived safely back on the earth after a four-day return journey.

The Modern Space Program

Six manned lunar missions followed the triumph of Apollo 11. Astronauts collected more moon rocks for study on earth. They left a set of mirrors there which is used to this day for measuring the distance from the earth to the moon by clocking the round-trip travel-time of a laser beam reflected from the mirrors. The astronauts also left a series of seismographs to detect and measure lunar quakes.

The last manned trip to the moon was in 1972. NASA is now proposing another manned lunar mission in the next few years. By the time you read these lines, that mission may have become reality.

After the highly successful series of manned lunar missions in the 1960s and 1970s, NASA turned its focus to the development of a space station. Work also began on the development of the space shuttle. This was to be a reusable vehicle that would ferry people and supplies to the space station, then return to earth as a glider, where it could be launched again. NASA launched the first space shuttle, the Columbia, in 1981. NASA now has a fleet of space shuttles, most of which have been reused many times.

While the Americans worked on shuttle technology, the Soviets developed a space station named Mir. Individual Soviet astronauts have now spent several months and more at Mir on several occasions.

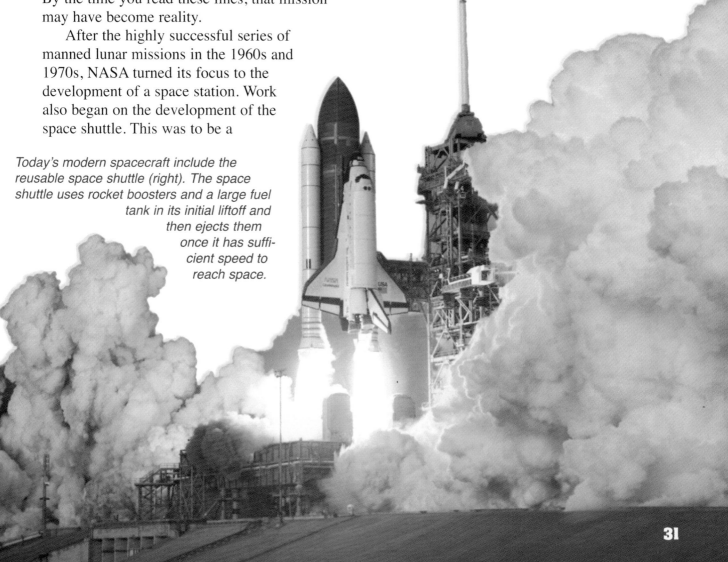

Today's modern spacecraft include the reusable space shuttle (right). The space shuttle uses rocket boosters and a large fuel tank in its initial liftoff and then ejects them once it has sufficient speed to reach space.

Unmanned Missions

Both the space shuttle research and the research at Mir have turned up unexpected difficulties. The space shuttles have tended to degrade with each launch, resulting in unpredictable failures and a lack of dependability.

At the Mir space station, the Soviets found that astronauts living in the weightlessness of space for long periods suffer from physical degradation. The astronauts lose calcium from their bones making bone fractures likely. Their muscles become weak, and after a term of several months on Mir, an astronaut must be taken out on a stretcher to a hospital for recovery and exercise.

Because of the problems with long-term shuttle use and long-term missions on Mir, the attention of space scientists has turned back to short-term manned missions.

Unmanned missions performed by remote control are also much in the plans of space scientists. The most famous unmanned mission to date was the journey of the Voyager 2 probe through the outer solar system.

The Voyager 2 spacecraft, shown above, sent back detailed photos and information about the solar system. The spacecraft is still traveling through the outer solar system and beyond.

The Voyager 2 probe was launched in 1977. It was fitted with a television camera which was computer-controlled from the earth.

Though earlier unmanned probes had been

Manned missions, such as the Mir space station (above) and the space shuttle (below) have very limited reach into space because of the long term effects of space on humans.

sent to the moon, Mars, Venus, and Mercury, Voyager 2 was more remarkable than any of them. From 1977 to 1989, Voyager 2 took photographs and videos of

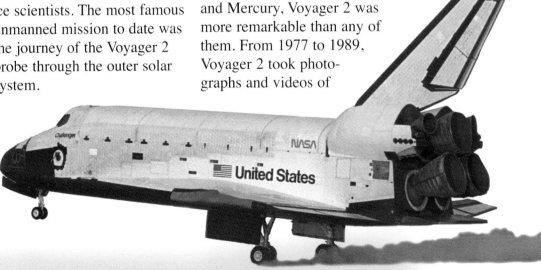

Jupiter, Saturn, Uranus, and Neptune which were much better than any images ever seen through telescopes. Planets which had never been seen clearly were now visible in crisp, clear color videos. Moons which had never been seen as more than points of light took on unique features and colors.

All of these stunning photographs and videos are in the public domain. NASA has not copyrighted them, and they are available from NASA libraries around the country. There is a modest fee for some items. For more information, you can write to NASA Education Division, Washington, DC.

The Viking orbiter/lander was an unmanned mission to Mars that took photos from the atmosphere and from the surface of Mars.

This montage of Saturn and her moons is made of photos from the Voyager mission.

What Has the Space Program Taught Us?

As long as Dr. von Braun was scientific chief at NASA, the scientists and astronauts there, including Dr. von Braun himself, commonly credited the Lord Jesus Christ for making their achievements possible, and acknowledged the Creator's works in the heavens.

In 1977, however, Dr. von Braun passed away, sadly bringing his outspoken Christian testimony to an end. Despite NASA's evolutionary shift after von Braun's death, space research has consistently pointed to creation and away from evolution. We will examine some of these exciting developments in the following chapters.

Dr. von Braun was a brilliant scientist who was able to see God in all of the creation around him. He helped lead the NASA space agency and gave God the glory for its achievements.

Space Highlights

1957 First artificial satellite, Sputnik, October 4

1958 First American satellite, Explorer, January 31

1961 First man in space, Yuri Gagarin, April 12

1961 First American in space, Alan Shepard, May 5

1962 First American to orbit the earth, John Glenn, February 20

1968 First flight to the moon; astronauts photographed the moon from tens of miles without landing; backside of the moon televised to the earth, December 24

1969 First moon landing; Neil Armstrong, followed by Edwin Aldrin, set foot on the moon, July 20

1970   Apollo 13 moon mission aborted due to oxygen tank failure, April

1976   First Mars lander, Viking probe, arrives on Mars, July 20

1977   Voyager 2 launched, August 20

1981   First reusable spacecraft, space shuttle Columbia, launched April 12

1990   First space telescope, Hubble Space Telescope, launched

1995   First sampling of Jupiter's atmosphere; Galileo probe arrives at Jupiter

1997   First mobile remote probe on any planet; Rover probe explores Martian surface

Chapter 7

A Tour of the Solar System

The Earth: Not Just Another Planet

Our tour of the solar system starts with our home, the earth. The earth is the only inhabited planet in the solar system. This sets the earth apart as special. Though the earth is one of the smaller planets, at only one-thousandth the size of the largest planet, Jupiter, the Bible never presents the earth as small in God's sight. According to God's Word, the earth is the most important place in the solar system.

Moon

Isaiah 45:18 says of the earth that God "formed it to be inhabited." This claim is made of no other place anywhere. Furthermore, space probes have turned up zero evidence of life elsewhere, confirming that the earth is unique.

Of all the heavenly bodies, the earth was the first to be created (Gen. 1:1). God made all the other heavenly bodies on day four of the creation week, but only the earth was made on day one. Even in the creation week, God set the earth apart as unique, not just another planet.

The earth is also unique in its distance from the sun. On Mercury and Venus, closer to the sun than the earth, the heat is scorching and the temperatures are deadly hot. For all the planets farther from the sun than the earth, the sun's heat is too dim and the planets are too cold to support life. Only the earth is placed to receive a comfortable level of light and heat from the sun.

The earth is the only planet with any liquid water at all. Oceans of liquid water cover over 70 percent of the earth's surface. The earth, sometimes nicknamed the "Blue Planet" because of the blue color of the oceans, is the only place in the entire universe known to have liquid water. Life absolutely must have liquid water to survive, and the earth is uniquely designed with vast reservoirs of this life-sustaining fluid.

The earth (above) is the only known place in the universe that can sustain life. God placed the earth at the perfect distance from the sun to provide the right amount of heat and light.

Jupiter

Relative size of Earth

The earth is 1,000 times smaller than the largest planet, Jupiter, but God saw it as so important that He created it on day one of the creation week. The other planets were not created until day four.

Why Did God Make Other Planets?

Pluto

I f the other planets do not support life of their own, why do they exist? There is the time-telling purpose of all the heavenly bodies (Gen. 1:14–18). Planets are included in this purpose as "stars" in Genesis 1:16. Another purpose for the planets is that they act together to stabilize the solar system, a fact discovered by the French atheist Laplace in the 1790s.

Mercury

Mars

God created each one of the planets in a special way, each one with a special size, gravity, chemical makeup, rotation rate, magnetism, and axis tilt. Each one of these special properties of the planets helps to keep the solar system stable and safe. In particular, the other planets stabilize the distance of the earth from the sun.

They keep the earth from approaching too close or moving too far from the sun. This ensures the ability of the earth to support life.

Venus

Astronomers who believe in cosmic evolution think that all the special properties of each planet developed by chance. According to this idea, there should be a way to explain how each planet came to have its own special rotation rate, axis tilt, and other properties.

Uranus

However, we will see evidence from astronomy which shows that the planets were created with these special properties in the beginning.

God created each of the planets in the exact way that would support the earth in a stable solar system. All nine planets are shown above in their sizes compared to each other. Jupiter is the largest planet (left), and Pluto is the smallest (top right).

Neptune

The Moon: A Special Satellite

The moon is about one-eightieth the mass of the earth. Its gravity is one-sixth as strong as the earth's gravity. If you weigh 120 pounds on earth, you would weigh only 20 pounds on the moon.

There is no air or liquid water on the moon, so astronauts traveling to the moon must wear spacesuits. Even with a heavy spacesuit on, lunar astronauts have no trouble jumping six feet high in the low gravity.

Because there is no air

on the moon, there is no blue sky. The lunar sky is always pitch black, even at midday. Without an atmosphere to protect the lunar surface, daytime temperatures reach 250°F (120°C), and nighttime lows plunge to -250°F (-160°C). The moon turns on its axis once every 29 ½ days*, so it bakes for nearly 2 weeks, then freezes for 2 weeks. Unlike the earth, the moon cannot support life.

The moon appears red during a lunar eclipse (left) next to the earth with a distant star behind.

Earth

239,000 miles.

The Origin of the Moon

For many years, some scientists have supposed that the moon evolved from the same materials of which the earth is made. Genesis chapter 1 contradicts this idea.

Genesis 1:14 states that God spoke to bring about the creation of the heavenly bodies. Genesis 1:16 mentions the moon as one of these heavenly bodies. Genesis 1:19 tells us that these heavenly bodies were created on day four. Yet the earth was created on day one, so the earth had already existed for three days when God created the moon. Thus, the moon and the earth did not come from the same material.

This has been confirmed by the moon rocks brought back to the earth by lunar astronauts. Scientists who have carefully analyzed the moon rocks have found that they have a very different chemical composition from earth rocks. It is clear that earth rocks and moon rocks did not evolve together. God created the earth and the moon separately and independently of each other.

The moon as photographed by the Galileo spacecraft at about 350,000 miles.

*Relative to the earth's surface.

How Old Is the Moon?

Lunar missions have provided a fascinating answer to this question. Using mirrors left on the surface of the moon by lunar astronauts, scientists have been able to measure the distance to the moon with extreme precision.

always been happening as it is today, the moon has moved some 1,000 feet away from the earth. This is less than one mile, and is only a very small fraction of the moon's distance of 239,000 miles from us.

But some astronomers believe that the moon is nearly 5 billion years old. In 5 billion years, the moon would have receded 2 billion feet, or 300,000 miles*. If this had happened, the moon would no longer have the same orbit around the earth. This means that the moon cannot be billions of years old.

By using mirrors left on the moon's surface by astronauts, astronomers can precisely measure its distance to the earth. The moon is moving away from the earth about two inches a year.

Moon

A lunar rock from the Apollo 15 mission

The distance to the moon is now known to within one inch.

Astronomers have found that the moon is moving away from the earth little by little. This is called "lunar recession." Every year, the moon is about two inches farther from the earth than the year before. In other words, the moon is "receding" from the earth a little bit each year.

In the 6,000 years or so since creation, if lunar recession has

* Hypothetical recession over alleged 5 billion years is more than two inches per year.

The Sun, a Light-Giver

God has given the sun a special purpose. It is the "great light" for the earth (Gen. 1:16). However, the sun is not the ultimate giver of light and life.

Genesis chapter 1 tells us that God created the sun on day four of the creation week, three days after He created the earth on day one. God on day four designed the sun to be the source of light for the earth. Yet before the sun existed, the earth experienced day and night (Gen. 1:5, 8, 13), possibly with God himself being the source of light.

The sun is by far the largest object in the solar system. It is nearly one million miles across, and more than 300,000 times heavier than the earth. One million earth-size planets could fit inside the sun.

The sun is a very hot ball of gas. The average temperature of the surface is about 10,000°F (6,000°C). At this temperature, the gases of the sun glow with heat much like a hot stove unit. Some parts of the surface are somewhat cooler than others. The cooler parts look dark in contrast with the hotter areas, and they are called "sunspots." Sunspots appear to be small black circles on the sun, but the smallest sunspot is several times the size of the earth.

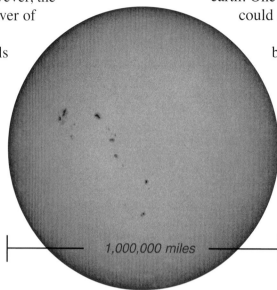

The sun is a hot ball of gas with a surface temperature of about 10,000°F. Sunspots are cooler areas on the surface which appear as dark regions.

1,000,000 miles

The Sun: Not Just Another Star

The sun is the only star in the solar system. Yet it is not just another average star. The sun is unusual in several ways. Unlike most stars, for instance, the sun is isolated.

Most stars are members of systems of two or more stars. One example of such a star system is the Alpha Centauri system. Long thought to be a single star in isolation, Alpha Centauri is surrounded by other dimmer stars which are invisible to all but the most powerful telescopes. In fact, most stars that appear to be single to the unaided eye are in systems with other dimmer stars.

If the earth were in this kind of star system, life probably could not survive. With other nearby stars in the system tugging and pulling on the earth, the earth would at some times be so close to the sun as to literally broil all living things. At other times the earth would be so far away that all life would freeze.

But the sun is not part of any star system. The unusual isolation of the sun makes it a predictable giver of light and heat, and a predictable time-teller for life

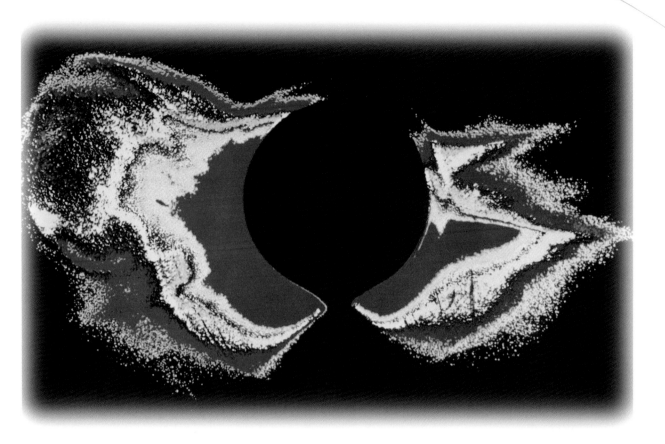

The sun is unusual because it gives off a relatively constant amount of energy (above). The energy output of most stars varies drastically, making life around them impossible. The different colors around the sun (darkened) show the energy radiating from the sun.

on the earth — the very purposes specified for it in Genesis 1:14-18.

Another property of most stars but not for the sun, is an extremely changeable or "variable" energy output. Many stars are unstable. Their energy output is always changing. They are sometimes very hot, and other times relatively cool.

Life would be impossible around a variable star. But the sun's energy output is constant to within a few tenths of one percent, a fact which has led some astronomers to call it the "constant sun."

A view of solar ultraviolet radiation

A solar flare on the sun (left) gives off large amounts of energy. A large flare can disrupt communications satellites on Earth.

Where Does the Sun Get Its Heat?

Scientists have long realized that there is no air in outer space, so the sun could not be an ordinary burning fuel like coal or pitch.

In the 1870s the German physicist Hermann von Helmholtz proposed that the sun is shrinking. He claimed that the sun is giving off energy as it shrinks. This process could account for all the sun's energy output for millions of years, far longer than the sun has actually been operating, based on the biblical age of the creation.

By Helmholtz' time, however, some scientists believed that the solar system must be hundreds of millions, if not billions, of years old. To them, the sun would have to last this long for the solar system to evolve. They were not satisfied with Helmholtz' idea of solar shrinkage, because it did not provide enough time for the evolution of the solar system.

German physicist Hermann von Helmholtz proposed that the sun was giving off energy as it shrank in size. Today, scientists can measure the shrinkage.

For many years this remained a problem for evolutionary theorists. Then came the discovery of radioactivity and nuclear physics. In the 1920s some scientists claimed that nuclear reactions were going on in the sun.

According to this idea, the main nuclear reaction is the combination or "nuclear fusion" of four atoms of hydrogen into one atom of helium, together with the release of a huge amount of energy. With nuclear fusion, the sun could function for over 10 billion years before burning out.

But is the sun really getting its energy from nuclear fusion? The evidence says no. As hydrogen fuses into helium, not only energy but very tiny particles called "neutrinos" should be produced. Scientists have worked very hard to detect the neutrinos the sun should be producing from nuclear fusion. However, they have found only one-half the expected number of neutrinos. This means that, at best, nuclear fusion produces only part of the sun's energy.

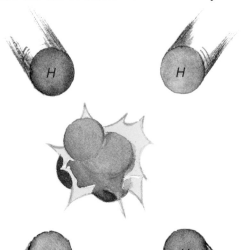

Nuclear fusion is the process of hydrogen atoms fusing together to form helium atoms. In the process it releases large amounts of energy. While this process may be part of the sun's energy, evidence more strongly supports von Helmholtz' idea of solar shrinkage.

How Old Is the Sun?

There is evidence that the sun is, and always has, produced energy by shrinkage just as Helmholtz proposed. What is this evidence?

At Greenwich Observatory, the noonday passage of the sun has been observed daily for almost 200 years. A by-product of these observations is that they have given a daily record of the size of the sun. The size of the sun has shown a steady decrease over the decades.

Thus, the sun is shrinking and is generating most, maybe all, of its energy by shrinkage. The same might be true for other stars, too. This means that, as Helmholtz said in the 1870s, the sun has a maximum lifetime of millions of years, not enough time for the evolution of the solar system, but more than enough time for the sun to have given light since the creation week.

Astronomers have carefully measured the shrinking of the sun for almost 200 years. The rate of shrinkage fits perfectly into the time span of creation, but contradicts evolution.

The Nebular Hypothesis: A False Idea

Most astronomers who believe in evolution claim that the solar system evolved from a cloud of gas and dust. This gas and dust is supposedly material produced by the big bang.

The sun, and all the moons and planets, allegedly formed over billions of years as the gas and dust particles came together to make the solar system the way it is today.

According to this idea, each moon and planet formed along similar lines. No moon or planet should be too different from any other. They should all conform to a single pattern. This evolutionary idea is called the "nebular hypothesis."

The phrase "nebular hypothesis" comes from the word nebula, the Latin word for "cloud." Most scientists who believe in the nebular hypothesis believe that the solar system is about 5 billion years old.

Many people believe that the solar system evolved from a gas cloud after the big bang (left). Astronomy does not support this idea, called the "nebular hypothesis." The nebular hypothesis is a false idea.

Mercury and Venus

Mercury and Venus are both closer to the sun than the earth, and they both have red-hot surfaces with none of the liquid water required for life.

Mercury is one of the smallest planets at less than half the size of the earth. Space probes have returned data from Mercury showing that it has a very large metallic core, presumably iron. Why is this significant? Because the nebular hypothesis used to predict that Mercury, being a very small planet, might have no core at all.

But Mercury has one of the largest cores of any planet. This makes Mercury's composition unique. Mercury was created as is and did not evolve from a nebula along with any other planets.

Venus, the second planet out from the sun, has the hottest surface of any planet, even hotter than Mercury. This is because thick clouds of sulfuric acid and carbon dioxide cover the surface of Venus and trap the sun's heat. The clouds also make the surface invisible to ordinary earth-bound telescopes.

The clouds reflect nearly all the sunlight falling on them, making Venus the brightest planet in the sky, and the third brightest object in the heavens after the sun and the moon.

Sometimes it is possible to see Venus in the daytime.

The rotation of Venus is opposite to the other planets, disproving the nebular hypothesis.

Venus has the hottest surface of any planet. The red color shown is from the rocks glowing with heat, not from red pigments.

If you were on Venus and could see the sun coming up, it would come up in the west and set in the east. This is because Venus rotates backwards, or "retrograde." Most of the planets rotate "prograde" with the sun coming up in the east and setting in the west. Yet, if the nebular hypothesis were true, all the planets should have condensed with the same rotational direction out of the nebula. The retrograde rotation of Venus is a serious problem for the nebular hypothesis.

Astronomers used to claim that Venus did at first rotate prograde, but the earth somehow tugged on a hypothetical (imaginary) bulge on one side of Venus, forcing it into a retrograde rotation. But later observations showed that Venus is almost perfectly spherical. It is even rounder than

Although the surface of Mercury is very hot, it is dormant, without volcanic activity.

the earth. Venus has no bulges that the earth could have pulled on to slow Venus down and reverse its rotation. God created the rotation of Venus retrograde.

Mars: Not a Life-Supporting Planet

Beyond the earth is Mars. Mars is about 50 percent farther from the sun than the earth. It has temperatures that peak at about 70°F (20°C) in the Martian summertime, but the rest of the time the temperatures plunge as low as -150°F (-100°C). This is much colder than any place on the earth, much colder even than Siberia or the Antarctic.

Although people have long thought of Mars as supporting alien life, many expeditions to Mars, including the Rover mission, found nothing except dry deserts and rock (above).

It is tempting to compare Mars to the earth. Of all the planets, Mars is most similar to the earth. A day on Mars is 24 ½ hours, and the Martian year is only twice as long as a year on the earth. Mars is most like the earth of any planet.

However, the differences between Mars and the earth overshadow the similarities. Mars has no liquid water. It is drier than the driest desert on the earth. The Martian air is very thin. The air pressure on the surface of Mars is only one-fiftieth the air pressure at the top of Mt. Everest, the tallest mountain on the earth. Furthermore, Martian air is mostly carbon dioxide with very little oxygen. In other words, breathing Martian air would be almost like breathing car exhaust. Mars is no place for life.

Nevertheless, in 1976 an unmanned space probe named Viking landed on Mars to search for life. It found none.

The hopes for finding life on Mars have not died. In 1996, NASA announced that scientists had found "Mars rocks" in Antarctica which supposedly contained molecules made by living things. Further research revealed that these molecules were only inorganic and had never been associated with life.

This view of the Martian surface shows layers of carbon dioxide haze on the horizon. Carbon dioxide makes up most of the Martian atmosphere.

Furthermore, the Mars rocks themselves were not a new discovery. They were found a number of years ago. NASA's claim in 1996 that the rocks were evidence of Martian life happened just as Congress was debating whether to pay for a mission to Mars. As events worked out, Congress had approved a Martian "Rover" mission. On the Fourth of July, 1997, the Martian Rover arrived on Mars. It was the first remote-controlled probe ever sent to any planet, but it has found no evidence of life on Mars.

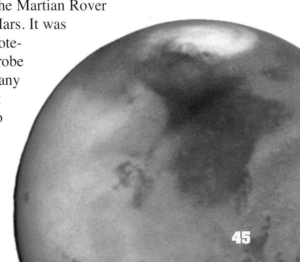

Jupiter and Saturn

oving out from Mars, we come to Jupiter, the giant planet one thousand times as big as the earth. In fact, Jupiter has more mass than all the other planets put together.

Perhaps the best way to visualize the huge size of Jupiter is to think about the depth of its atmosphere. The Galileo probe which reached Jupiter in 1995 penetrated several thousand miles into the atmosphere before it ceased sending data.

No one really knows the total depth of the gases on Jupiter, nor does anyone

Jupiter is no place for life. Its atmosphere is made of poisonous gases like ammonia, methane, and hydrogen. Jupiter's atmosphere has the longest-lasting storm in the entire solar system, a massive cyclone large enough to

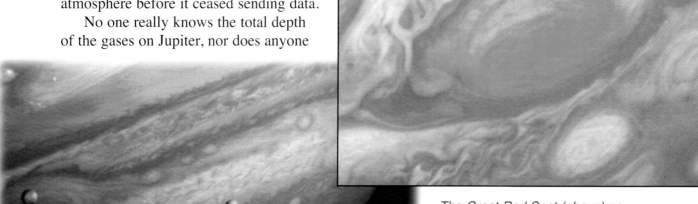

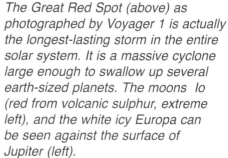

The Great Red Spot (above) as photographed by Voyager 1 is actually the longest-lasting storm in the entire solar system. It is a massive cyclone large enough to swallow up several earth-sized planets. The moons Io (red from volcanic sulphur, extreme left), and the white icy Europa can be seen against the surface of Jupiter (left).

know what is at the core of Jupiter. Jupiter may be nothing more than a big ball of gases. The gases are different shades of red, brown, orange, and yellow, giving Jupiter a colorful appearance visible from earth-based telescopes.

This montage of Jupiter (right) and its moons Io, Europa, Ganymede, and Callisto, was made of photos from Voyager 2.

swallow up several earth-size planets. It is called the "Great Red Spot," and is at least as old as the first view of it in the 1600s.

Out beyond Jupiter is Saturn, the "ringed planet." Saturn's famous rings are not unique. Jupiter, Uranus, and Neptune also have rings, but Saturn's rings are the widest and were the first to be discovered, by Galileo in the early 1600s.

Poisonous Gases on Jupiter and Saturn

Gas	Found on Earth
1. **Ammonia**	used for cleaning
2. **Methane**	swamp gas
3. **Hydrogen**	explosive fuel
4. **Oxides of Nitrogen**	smog

Saturn a very colorful appearance as seen by Voyager 2 in 1981.

One of the largest moons of Saturn is Titan. Unlike most moons, Titan has an atmosphere. Titan's atmosphere shows that Titan must be young. Though large, as moons go, Titan is less massive than all the planets except Pluto, and it has only a small gravitational field. If it were billions of years old, its atmosphere would have escaped from its small gravitational pull long ago.

Like Jupiter, Saturn has a very thick atmosphere made of poisonous gases, and like Jupiter, Saturn may be simply a big gas ball. The gases are colored various shades of brown, yellow, red, and green, giving

Unlike other moons, Titan (left), one of Saturn's largest moons, has an atmosphere. Because of Titan's low gravity, the moon must be very young or else the atmosphere would have already escaped.

Uranus and Neptune

Out beyond Saturn is Uranus. Like Jupiter and Saturn, Uranus remains a mystery planet because a poisonous atmosphere thousands of miles thick obscures

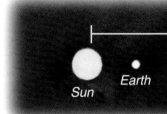

the nebular hypothesis. The nebular hypothesis cannot account for the retrograde rotation of Uranus. Uranus was created as is.

There is another way in which Uranus does not fit the nebular hypothesis. The nebular hypothesis predicts that all planets should have axes tilted at similar angles. With most planets, the axis is tilted similarly to the 23 $\frac{1}{2}$ degrees for the earth's axis. Yet the axis of Uranus is tilted 98 degrees. How could this be explained without resorting to the idea that the axis of Uranus was created as is?

Some scientists used to claim that there was a collision that upset the axis of Uranus. But in 1986 the Voyager 2 probe came within a few thousand miles of Uranus and its moons.

Uranus is tilted on its side and rotates backwards compared to the other planets. Its faint rings and some of its moons can also be seen in the photo above.

whatever might lie below. The atmosphere is mostly a deep blue-green with a few patches of white and black.

Like Venus, Uranus rotates retrograde. Voyager 2 confirmed this. As with Venus, the retrograde rotation is a serious problem for

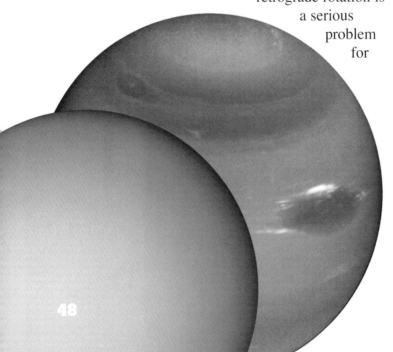

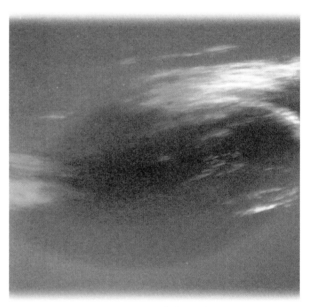

The giant spot on Neptune (above) is believed to be a violent storm similar to the Great Red Spot on Jupiter.

Voyager 2 confirmed that all of Uranus' largest moons lie in precisely circular orbits in the plane of Uranus' equator. The orbits of the moons are not random such as a collision would produce. Evidently, the Uranian system has not been disturbed. The axis tilt of 98 degrees did not result from a collision. It was created as is.

Out beyond Uranus is Neptune, first seen at close range by the Voyager 2 probe in 1989. It has a very thick atmosphere made of gases colored a deep blue.

One of the features revealed by Voyager 2 was the "Great Dark Spot" in Neptune's atmosphere, similar to the Great Red Spot on Jupiter. Both of these seem to be very violent storms, indicating the harshness of these planets for any kind of life.

Pluto

4,000,000,000 miles

Pluto

Illustration of Charon

The most distant known planet is Pluto. Pluto is four billion miles from the sun. In comparison, the earth is about 100 million miles from the sun, one-fortieth the distance of Pluto. At Pluto's distance from the earth, Pluto looks like a speck of light in all but the most powerful telescopes such as the Hubble Space Telescope. It was not even discovered until 1930.

Pluto can be seen to the left and its moon, Charon, on the right in this Hubble Space Telescope image.

Pluto has a moon of its own. This moon is named Charon (pronounced "CARE-on"). The Hubble Space Telescope has returned some fairly good images of Pluto and Charon.

Before the discovery of Charon in 1978, many astronomers had considered Pluto to be an escaped moon of Neptune. There was only

one reason for this: Pluto is not like the other outer planets. Jupiter, Saturn, Uranus, and Neptune are gigantic "gas balls" with atmospheres thousands of miles thick, but Pluto has hardly any atmosphere at all.

The nebular hypothesis had predicted that all the outer planets should have very thick atmospheres, but Pluto does not fit this pattern.

Since Pluto has a moon of its own, it is obviously a planet. The difference between Pluto and the other outer planets shows that when God spoke the planets into existence, He made them each unique and different.

Artist's conception of Pluto

49

Chapter 8

STARS AND GALAXIES

On a clear night far from city lights, you can see about 2,000 stars. However, the stars in the sky change with the seasons. World travelers have also noticed that a change of geographical location brings different stars into view. With seasonal and geographical changes, about 6,000 stars are visible to the unaided eye.

Using the first telescopes in the early 1600s, astronomers saw millions of stars for the first time, not just the 6,000 or so previously visible.

Astronomers now estimate that there are billions and billions of stars visible through powerful telescopes. Amazingly, God describes the creation of all these stars in only one phrase. The last part of Genesis 1:16 says, "He made the stars also." Yet the creation of the earth and its life takes up nearly all the first chapter of Genesis. Evidently, God considers the earth more important than all the stars.

Astronomers estimate that there are billions and billions of stars, but without a telescope, only about 6,000 in all are visible. The movement of the stars around the North Star can be seen in the long exposure photo below.

What Are Stars Made Of?

Stars shine because the elements in them are glowing with heat. Scientists say that the elements are "incandescent." Each element in stars shines with a unique spectrum of colors. The spectrum of colors for each element is like a "fingerprint." The spectrum of the element identifies it. Astronomers can examine the spectrum of any incandescent material to know exactly which elements are in it.

spectral classes as the initial letters of words in the sentence, Oh Be A Fine Girl — Kiss Me — Smack! The sun is a class G star.

Amazingly, no star has been found with different spectral "fingerprints" from the elements on the earth. Every element occurring naturally on the earth has also been detected in the stars. Stars do not have any exotic, extraterrestrial elements.

This occurrence of the same elements

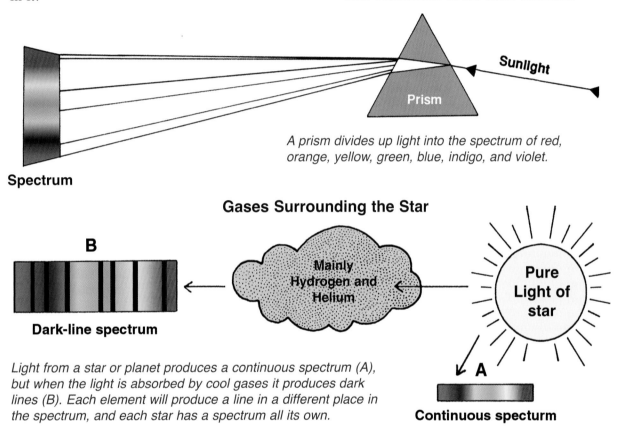

Spectrum

A prism divides up light into the spectrum of red, orange, yellow, green, blue, indigo, and violet.

Gases Surrounding the Star

B

Dark-line spectrum

Pure Light of star

A

Continuous specturm

Light from a star or planet produces a continuous spectrum (A), but when the light is absorbed by cool gases it produces dark lines (B). Each element will produce a line in a different place in the spectrum, and each star has a spectrum all its own.

This so-called "spectral analysis" has been done for thousands of stars. Most stars are about 75 percent hydrogen and 25 percent helium, with about 1 percent of other elements. However, the composition of no two stars is exactly the same.

Astronomers have grouped stars into "spectral classes" based on temperature and composition. These spectral classes are O, B, A, F, G, K, M, and S. You can remember the

throughout the heavens is a testimony to the omniscience of the Creator, who is mighty enough to make and sustain His universe with the same kinds of elements everywhere. If the cosmos had evolved, we would expect to see that different kinds of elements had evolved in different places. Some stars would have spectral "fingerprints" different from any elements on the earth.

Stars Are Not All the Same

S ky watchers have long noticed that some
stars are dim and others are bright.
Around 130 B.C., the Greek astronomer
Hipparchus established a system for grouping
stars by brightness.

In Hipparchus' system, the brightest stars
were said to have a magnitude of 1. The
dimmest stars visible to the unaided eye had a
magnitude of 6. The dimmer the star, the higher the magnitude. The brighter the star, the
lower the magnitude.

With a few changes, modern astronomers
still use this system of "stellar magnitudes."
Telescopes can see stars dimmer than a magnitude of 6. The dimmest visible celestial
objects have magnitudes of about 30. On the

*In 130 B.C. Hipparchus, the Greek astronomer,
established a system for grouping stars by brightness. Astronomers still use a system similar to his
today, to classify stars by their magnitude.*

other end of the scale, a few of the brightest
stars have magnitudes less than zero.

The brightest heavenly object of all, the
sun, has a magnitude of -26.5. The brightest
star is Sirius with a magnitude of -1.4.

Magnitude of Heavenly Bodies

Object	Magnitude
Sun	-26.5
Full Moon	-12.5
Venus	-4.4
Mars	-2.7
Jupiter	-2.6
Sirius (brightest star)	-1.4
Bright Asteroid	6
Limit of Human Vision *	6
Pluto	15

* The faintest star that can be seen with the human eye.

*The chart above shows the
different magnitudes for
some heavenly objects.*

*The star Betelgeuse
(middle) is one million times
larger than our sun. If it was
in our solar system, it would
cover Mercury, Venus,
Earth, and Mars. Betelgeuse
is in the upper left shoulder
of the constellation Orion
(right).*

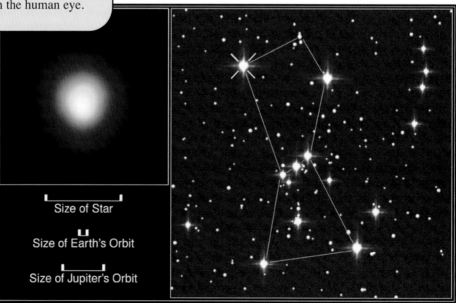

Size of Star

Size of Earth's Orbit

Size of Jupiter's Orbit

Stars have different colors, different temperatures, different chemical compositions, different rates of rotation, and different sizes. One of the largest stars, for instance, is Betelgeuse, about 600 light-years away.

Betelgeuse is about 1 million times larger than the sun. If Betelgeuse were in our solar system, it is so big that it would cover Mercury, Venus, and Earth. It would reach beyond Mars. At the other extreme are white dwarfs, much heavier than any planet, but only around 1 percent the size of the sun.

Do Black Holes Exist?

A black hole is supposedly a celestial object so massive that nothing can escape from it, not even light or other radiation. This means that no astronomer has ever seen, or can hope to see, a black hole.

Since black holes cannot be seen, we must ask, "What are believers in black holes really observing?" Black holes supposedly pull in huge amounts of matter from the space surrounding them. According to this idea, cosmic matter speeding toward a black hole becomes extremely hot and begins to give off X-rays.

Yet there are many ordinary celestial objects which give off X-rays. Even the sun produces some X-rays, and many stars give off large amounts of X-rays. "X-ray sources," as they are called, are common. Believers in

Black holes are supposedly so massive that nothing can escape their pull of gravity, not even light or other radiation.

black holes assume that some of these X-ray sources must be black holes.

Since most X-ray sources are known to be ordinary stars, what is the reason for assuming that any X-ray source is due to a black hole which, by definition, can never be seen?

The answer is that black holes are considered to be the final stage of "stellar evolution" for some stars. Since the evolution of stars has never been observed, and black holes can never be observed, a belief in black holes is really based on the "evidence of things not seen" (Heb. 11:1).

The Closest Galaxies

The stars closest to us are the ones in the Milky Way Galaxy where our solar system is located. In clear country air, the stars of the Milky Way look like a white stream spilled across the sky, like milk poured from a bottle. The ancient Greeks thought of this similarity, and the name "Milky Way" has continued ever since. Our modern term "galaxy" in fact comes from the Greek for "milk."

There are several other large groups of stars near the Milky Way. The Large Magellanic Cloud, for

distances than single stars could ever be. They reveal the size of the universe, and therefore the power of God, in a way that single stars cannot.

The Andromeda Galaxy is the most distant object that can be seen without a telescope.

The nearest independent galaxy outside the Milky Way is the Andromeda Galaxy at a distance of some 2 million light-years. This means that light traveling at its present speed would take 2 million years to reach us from the Andromeda Galaxy. The Andromeda Galaxy is the most distant object that can be seen without a telescope.

The Milky Way Galaxy (above) in which we live got its name because the band of stars that we can see from Earth look like spilled milk.

example, contains several million stars and is considered part of the Milky Way complex. This structure is about 170,000 light-years away from us.

The Large Magellanic Cloud is one of the few objects outside the immediate vicinity of the Milky Way which can be seen without a telescope. This fact points to a special purpose for galaxies. Galaxies are visible from greater

The Large Magellanic Cloud contains several million stars and even though it is 170,000 light years away, it can be seen without a telescope.

Seeing Distant Objects in a Young Universe

How can astronomers see objects millions or billions of light-years away if the universe is only a few thousand years old? There is evidence that the speed of light was much higher in the past,[2] which means that the light we now see from the Andromeda Galaxy did not actually need 2 million years to reach us, but only a few thousand years.

The most distant galaxies are billions of light-years away in terms of the present speed of light. As with Andromeda, however, the higher speed of light in the past means that we see them today as they were only a few thousand years ago, not billions of years ago.

God not only created the stars themselves, but also filled space with their light, so that Adam and Eve and their children saw the heavens filled with stars. The stars were visible to be used as time-tellers from the beginning.

Adam and Eve would have seen a full sky of stars because God created the stars and filled the sky with their light.

Look-Back Time

God created the cosmos without any imperfections, yet today astronomers see many exploding stars millions of light-years away, and other catastrophes billions of light-years away. Yet the universe is only thousands of years old, not billions. These catastrophes, though not created by God, have become visible to astronomers on earth in only a few thousand years.

Astronomers who believe in cosmic evolution say this is not true. They claim that light from the most distant galaxies needed billions of years to reach earth, and they conclude that the universe must therefore be billions of years old.

When astronomers see extremely distant galaxies, they are seeing them as they were long ago when the light left them to begin its journey to earth. In other words, the astronomers are looking back in time. Astronomers call this "look-back" time.

Since the universe is truly 6,000 years old or so, the look-back time for even the most distant galaxies is 6,000 years or less. The catastrophes which astronomers observe in distant galaxies happened thousands of years ago, not billions.

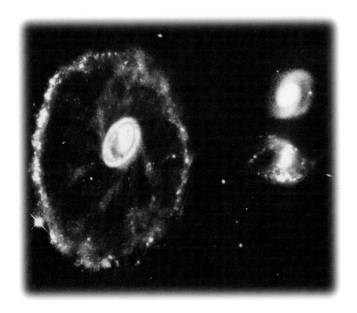

When astronomers see an exploding star (left), they are seeing it as it happened thousands of years ago.

Chapter 9

COSMIC CATASTROPHES

When God created the universe, it was perfect. Then sin entered into the creation by man's disobedience. Ever since, sin has caused death and decay on the earth. Natural events involving destruction, decay, and death are a major part of scientific research.

The cosmos has also suffered from sin. The universe is not the same as when God made it. Romans 8:22 tells us that the entire creation is now groaning because of the curse of sin. Every part of the universe has experienced some destructive change.

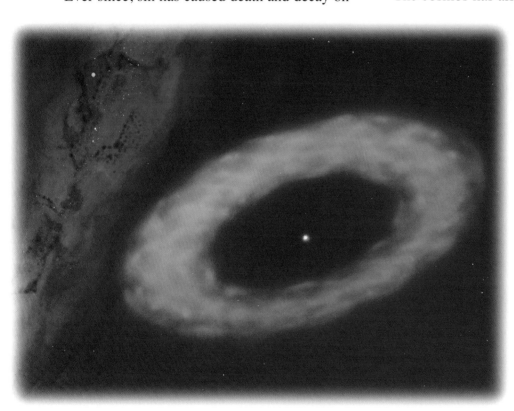

The Ring Nebula is a huge cloud of gases formed by the explosion of the star in the center of the picture.

Star Death

All stars are dying. They are burning out. With enough time, they would eventually be cold and dark. How long would this take?

The brightest stars, classed as O and B stars, could generate heat and light for ten million years or so at the most. After that, these stars would be cold and dark.

Yet there are many O and B stars still shining brightly. This shows that the universe cannot be ten million years old, and certainly not billions of years old as some astronomers claim.

Astronomers who believe in cosmic evolution are not satisfied with this conclusion. They claim that burned-out stars are replaced by new stars forming by "stellar evolution." But no one has ever seen a star form. The death of stars is final. They are not replaced.

The Death of the Sun

Even the sun is very self-destructive. On the sun there are huge explosions of super-hot gas called "solar prominences" and "solar flares" which shoot out half a million miles from the sun, spilling solar matter into space. The sun is losing multiplied tons of matter every day, besides the energy it radiates. It is slowly dying.

Scientists have found that the sun is in constant vibration under the tremendously destructive forces of its energy output. It is stressed by continuous convulsions that would make any earthquake seem like nothing by comparison.

As strange as it may seem, the sun is much more stable than most stars. The sun's light and energy output is so predictable that we can depend on it without a second thought. This is not true for most stars. God has evidently preserved the sun so as to protect the earth and its life.

The sun frequently experiences huge explosions of super-hot gas called solar prominences and solar flares as seen in this infra-red (heat) image of the sun.

Supernova Remnants

Many stars every year die a sudden death by exploding. When this happens, the star flares up for a few weeks or months and is much brighter than normal. It is called a "nova," or if the explosion is extremely noticeable, a "supernova."

There are many remnants of the past destruction of stars.

When a star dies by exploding, it flares up much brighter for weeks or months. If the explosion is extremely noticeable, it is called a "supernova" (right).

For example, there is the Crab Nebula. Nebula (plural nebulae) is Latin for "cloud." In astronomy a nebula is any huge cloud of gas or dust in outer space, or any debris from stars, which looks like a fuzzy cloud at low telescope power.

The Crab Nebula is left over from a gigantic supernova explosion visible in A.D. 1054. Astronomers call it a "supernova remnant."

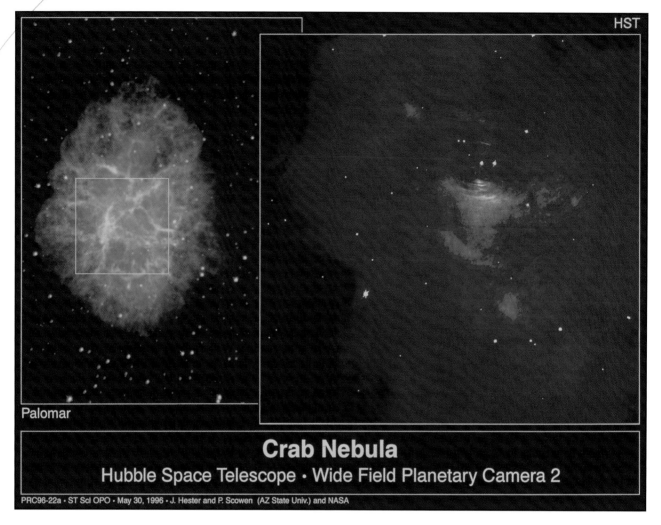

Palomar

Crab Nebula
Hubble Space Telescope · Wide Field Planetary Camera 2

PRC96-22a · ST ScI OPO · May 30, 1996 · J. Hester and P. Scowen (AZ State Univ.) and NASA

Astronomers have studied photographs of the Crab Nebula taken 14 years apart (in 1950 and 1964) to measure the expansion of the gas cloud away from the explosion. They found that the gases in the Crab Nebula are moving outward at thousands of miles an hour.

The Crab Nebula illustrates two general principles: (1) the gases in nebulae are expanding outward, not contracting inward; and (2) stars sometimes have been damaged very badly. Only a minority of stars, including the sun, have escaped severe destruction.

Today astronomers very rarely see new supernovas in our galactic neighborhood. Only three have been seen in over 400 years, one in 1572, another in 1604, and the most recent in 1987 in the Large Magellanic Cloud about 170,000 light-years away.

Since supernova sightings are very rare today, it follows that the most intense cosmic

The Crab Nebula is composed of leftover gases from a gigantic supernova that happened in A.D.1054. Astronomers have found that the gases in the nebula are expanding at thousands of miles an hour.

violence happened in the past. Perhaps this violence was the immediate reaction to the curse on the ground recorded in Genesis 3:17, which affected the entire universe.

Before sin entered into the universe, stars and all the rest of the creation functioned without violence. The creation was all "very good" (Gen. 1:31). But sin has made the creation break down. The stars which were made for God-ordained purposes, as specified in Genesis 1:14–18, have been destroying themselves.

The Myth of Star Birth

Though most stars do not disintegrate in supernova explosions, most stars are very unstable. These stars periodically eject clouds of gas into space on a scale that makes the solar prominences and solar flares of the sun look very small.

One example of such a damaged star is Betelgeuse (beetle-juice). Betelgeuse is a huge star about 600 light-years away with a diameter 700 times greater than the sun's. Every now and then Betelgeuse releases tremendous amounts of energy, causing the explosive ejection of some of its substance into a huge gas cloud which surrounds it. The gas cloud is continuously getting larger and is now one trillion miles across.

Like Betelgeuse, most stars are unstable. Some are called "variable stars" because their energy output is always changing. These stars are clearly dying because they are unstable. Yet some astronomers claim that observations of such stars are "proof" that the universe is evolving!

For example, there is beta-Pictoris, one of the most publicized cases of a star surrounded by a cloud of gas and dust. Some astronomers have claimed that a stellar system with planets (like our solar system) is somehow evolving from the cloud around Beta-Pictoris. There is no evidence for this.

Since all observed cosmic events are destructive, it is more reasonable to interpret the cloud as debris thrown off in partial explosions of this star.

Many stars are very unstable and eject large amounts of gas into space, filling each galaxy (below) with interstellar material.

Chapter 10

CATASTROPHES IN THE SOLAR SYSTEM

The solar system shows many signs of past catastrophes, one example being the rings of Saturn. The rings of Saturn are fragments of dust, rock, and ice. They apparently resulted from the explosion of one or more moons.

However, Saturn is not the only planet with rings. Jupiter has been found to have rings, but they are too narrow be seen from the earth. Voyager 2 first photographed them in 1979. Likewise, Uranus and Neptune both have narrow rings first seen by Voyager 2.

The rings of planets show that the catastrophes which formed them happened a few thousand years ago or less. In the more than 300 years since the rings of Saturn were discovered, astronomers have observed the rings becoming wider. The rings seem to be spreading out because of collisions between the particles in them.

How long would it be before the rings spread out so much that they are gone altogether? Calculations indicate about 10,000 years. Since the rings still exist, the catastrophe which formed the rings was not more than 10,000 years ago.

Astronomers who believe that the solar system is billions of years old have not been satisfied with this conclusion. They claim that there must be small moons existing within the rings with enough gravitational pull to keep the rings together. These hypothetical moons are called "shepherd moons."

The rings of Saturn have been expanding at a rate that shows that they could not have been formed more than a few thousand years ago.

According to this idea, the shepherd moons keep the ring particles together just as a shepherd rounds up the sheep in his flock. The biggest problem with the ring-confining moons is that they have not been observed.

Did Moons Really Explode?

The Five Major Moons of Uranus

Miranda

Ariel

Umbriel

Titania

Oberon

According to the nebular hypothesis, planetary rings are leftover material which failed to come together into moons during the alleged evolution of the solar system.

The nebular hypothesis is directly opposite of the idea that the rings came from the explosion of previously existing moons. If the nebular hypothesis were true, then every planet formed from gas and dust, and every planet should have rings of leftover debris.[3] Yet Mercury, Venus, the earth, and Mars have no rings at all, and Pluto, the outermost planet, probably does not.

Furthermore, the Bible tells us that God made a fully functioning and perfect universe in the creation week. The solar system did not begin as a chaotic cloud of rock and dust.

Not only is the nebular hypothesis false, but there is also evidence that moons actually did explode in the past. Some of Jupiter's moons have signs of massive stress and internal convulsions from the past, as if they almost melted or ruptured.

Several moons of Uranus, especially a moon called Miranda, are also very damaged. The surface of Miranda is warped and deformed, as if it were nearly torn apart by tremendous internal forces. Miranda is small, only 300 miles across, yet its surface has been so stressed that it has canyons 10 miles deep. This is ten times deeper than the Grand Canyon.

There are many signs of early catastrophes in Uranus' moons, such as Miranda (enlarged above) whose interior and surface have been severely damaged.

Astronomers have pointed out that a little additional stress might have made Miranda disintegrate. Furthermore, astronomers have pinpointed other moons which seem to have nearly fractured, such as Mimas, a moon of Saturn,[4] so it's likely that some moons really did come apart to form the rings of planets.

Of course, the earth has experienced the global flood of Noah, as well as regional catastrophes. Yet compared with Miranda, past catastrophes on the earth seem to have been relatively mild. If the earth had suffered the same level of violence as Miranda, all life might have been killed.

The Bible tells us in Isaiah 45:18 that God formed the earth to be inhabited. This has always been God's special purpose for the earth. To this end, God watched over life on the ark during the flood, as the Bible says in Genesis 8:1. It is clear that God has providentially cared for the earth to ensure that no terrestrial catastrophe would completely destroy the earth and its life.

What Are Asteroids?
Where Did They Come From?

A certain one-time planet between Mars and Jupiter apparently suffered even worse damage than Miranda. This planet evidently blew up, leaving the fragmented debris called the "asteroid belt." The asteroid belt is a great swarm of huge boulders, rocks, and pebbles between Mars and Jupiter.

Most asteroids are small. Even the largest one, Ceres, an oblong boulder about 400 miles long, is much smaller than any planet. Through a telescope the asteroids look like tiny points of light. They reminded astronomers of "little stars," the phrase

The asteroid Gaspra is shown above. The largest asteroids are only a few hundred miles long.

from which the Greek term asteroid was coined.

The first asteroid to be discovered was Ceres on New Year's Day 1801. Astronomers have now catalogued several thousand asteroids, which is only a small fraction of the millions (if not billions) of asteroids thought to exist.

Sometimes asteroids collide. When this happens, an asteroid may be knocked out of the asteroid belt altogether. The asteroid then can become a "meteor," a rock traveling randomly outside the asteroid belt.

Since the asteroid belt is constantly losing asteroids due to collisions, it would eventually disappear altogether. How long would this take? Based on the current rate of loss, the answer is about 10,000 years. In other words, the asteroid belt cannot be more than 10,000 years old.

Did a Planet Really Explode?

All the asteroids taken together weigh only $\frac{1}{2500}$ as much as the earth. There is no planet this small. Some astronomers have decided from this that the asteroids could not have come from the explosion of any planet.

However, in any explosion, most of the

debris leaves the site of the explosion forever. There are, in fact, minor belts of asteroids far outside the main asteroid belt. One of these is the Apollo asteroids, a swarm of boulders and other debris that sometimes comes close to the earth.

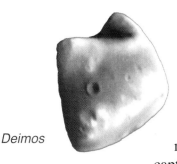

Deimos

Furthermore, some planets may have captured asteroids passing close by. Mars, for instance, has two small moons which appear to be captured asteroids. They are named Phobos and Deimos. Space probes have photographed both Phobos and some asteroids at very close range, confirming that they look quite similar.

Therefore, the mass of all the asteroids is much less than the mass of the planet that exploded to produce them. One notable astronomer concluded that the original planet may have been 90 times as large as the earth.[5]

An asteroid may collide with a moon or planet in an event called an "asteroid impact" or "meteor impact." On moons and planets with hard surfaces, the meteor impacts form craters which have been seen from the earth or by space probes. Mercury, Venus, the earth, the moon, and Mars, as well as the moons of other planets, all have meteor craters.

According to the nebular hypothesis, each moon and planet has grown from meteor impacts in all directions for billions of years. This

Two of Mars' moons, Deimos (left) and Phobos (below right), appear to be similar to other asteroids, such as Gaspra (facing page). Astronomers believe that they are both asteroids that were caught by Mars' gravity.

Mars

is how the moons and planets supposedly evolved to their present size. The nebular hypothesis claims that the asteroid belt is material left over from this process. The nebular hypothesis also claims that the craters on a moon or planet must be evenly spaced everywhere on the surface. Astronomers call this even spacing of craters "symmetrical cratering."

Astronomers have not observed symmetrical cratering anywhere. In fact, every moon and planet with craters has more craters in one hemisphere than the other. This shows that the nebular hypothesis is false.

Phobos

The earth, for example, has more craters in the Old World than the New World.[6] This situation is called "asymmetrical cratering," and is exactly what we would expect if a massive one-time planetary explosion had thrown debris through the solar system to hit whatever was in its path.

Every moon and planet has craters that are grouped more on one hemisphere than the other ("asymmetrical cratering," left). This is consistent with the theory of a planet that exploded in the young solar system.

Between Mars and Jupiter there is a ring of asteroids called the asteroid belt (left). Some astronomers believe that the planet that exploded to form them might have been 90 times as large as the earth.

Martian Catastrophes

All the planets with solid surfaces — Mercury, Venus, the earth, and Mars — show signs of violent past catastrophes, not enough to have destroyed them like the planet once between Mars and Jupiter, but enough to have left signs of damage. On Mars, for example, there is the Valles Marineris (the "Mariner Valley"), a canyon four times as deep and ten times as wide as the Grand Canyon.

Besides the Valles Marineris, Mars has the largest known volcano anywhere in the solar system. It is Olympus Mons ("Mount Olympus"), twice as high as Mount Everest and covering an area half as large as the state of Texas. Olympus Mons is now inactive, but it is testimony to the massive internal convulsions that once damaged Mars.

Mars is nicknamed the "Red Planet" because of its rusty red color, caused by iron oxide, rust, on its surface.

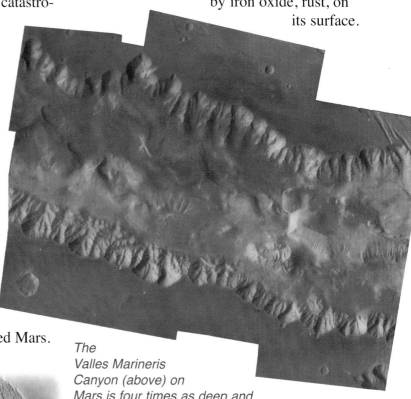

The Valles Marineris Canyon (above) on Mars is four times as deep and ten times as wide as the Grand Canyon (right) on the earth. This photo of the Candor Chasm region of Valles Marineris was taken by the Viking orbiter.

Ancient peoples associated its red color with blood and worshiped Mars as the god of war. But could there be a more literal reason for this association?

Could ancient peoples perhaps have seen violence on Mars? Some of these catastrophes, such as the eruptions of Olympus Mons, may have been visible to people on earth, leading them to associate violence and war with Mars.

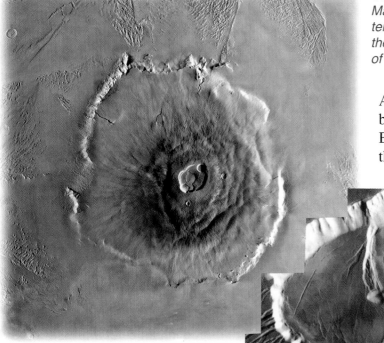

Olympus Mons (Mount Olympus) on Mars is the largest volcano in the solar system. It covers an area twice as large as Mount Everest and half the area of the state of Texas.

A closeup of the summit of Olympus Mons shows a vast volcanic crater, some fifty miles across and over 3,000 feet deep.

The Martian Flood

There are river canyons on Mars much like the Grand Canyon on the earth, only bigger. There must have been lots of liquid water flooding the Martian landscape to shape these canyons. The water apparently came from below the surface.

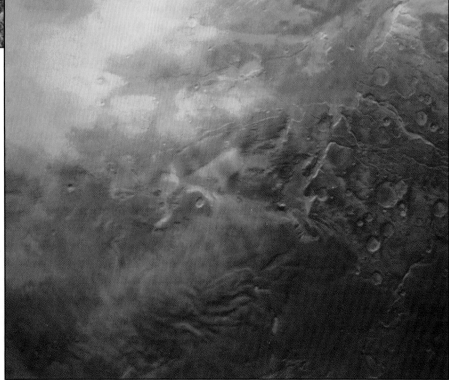

The Grand Canyon on the earth (above) is much smaller than the giant canyons on Mars.

There is no liquid water on Mars today. Astronomers have wondered where the water went. Most astronomers think that the water evaporated into the Martian atmosphere and eventually escaped into space. Now Mars is drier than the driest desert on the earth, so life cannot exist on Mars.

Most astronomers now believe that there was a nearly global flood on Mars. This is ironic, considering that many scientists continue to reject the reality of the global flood which happened on the earth.

The easy scientific acceptance of the Martian flood shows that Noah's flood is rejected not because of a lack of evidence, but because of the connection the Bible makes between Noah's flood and God's ability to judge sin.

Mars cannot support life today. However, before the ancient catastrophes, Mars may have been a better place. Though there is no evidence that life has ever existed on Mars, it does seem to have been more capable of potentially supporting life in the beginning. Perhaps the Creator intended Mars, in its more habitable original state, to be a "colonial outpost" for life traveling from earth.

There must have been massive amounts of flood waters on Mars to form the river channels seen on the surface below. The catastrophes happened in the past, because there is no water left on the surface today.

What Caused These Catastrophes? When Were They?

All the catastrophes we have discussed so far have something in common. They all seem to have been caused by a build-up of heat in moons and planets. Mars was certainly once much hotter internally than it is now. The past activity of Olympus Mons makes this very clear. Miranda, the moon of Uranus, was once hot enough internally to almost disintegrate. The moons which exploded to form rings, and the planet which exploded to form the asteroids, were heated internally to the point of disintegration.

The physical source of this heat is not certain. However, with few exceptions, even the existing planets and their moons, as well as the earth's moon, seem to have been hotter in the past.

The moon, and also Mercury and Venus, are partly covered by huge lava flows which are evidence of massive eruptions of hot rock in the past, though there are no active volcanoes known in any of these places today.

Furthermore, the three largest planets, Jupiter, Saturn, and Neptune, to this day are continuing to lose heat faster than they receive it from the sun. Voyager 2 measured the rate at which these planets are losing heat. In every case, if they had been losing heat at the present rate for more than a few thousand years, there would be no excess heat remaining. Therefore, the heat build-up in these planets happened only a few thousand years ago.

The nebular hypothesis also claims that the moons and planets were once very hot, but billions of years ago, not thousands. However, unlike the other outer planets, Uranus seems to be losing no heat today. Yet, according to the nebular hypothesis, these planets all formed in the same way under the same conditions. The drastic heat difference in Uranus compared with the other outer planets shows different internal behaviors and compositions which the nebular hypothesis cannot explain. Uranus and the other planets did not form from a common nebula. They were each uniquely created.

There is evidence, for the earth at least, that it was not hot in the beginning.[7] Genesis chapter 1 presents the newly created earth as cool and habitable originally, not hot and molten.

Therefore the heat build-up in the earth began after the creation week, presumably after the curse on the ground. The same could have been true for the other planets, their moons, and the earth's moon. Only later, perhaps around the time of the flood on earth some 5,000 years ago, did the heat build-up lead to the catastrophes we have been discussing.

Most of the catastrophes in the solar system occurred by a buildup of heat inside the planets and their moons, some to the point of disintegration. Even the layers of the earth show the internal heat typical of the planets, with a hot central core and a mantle of partly molten rock.

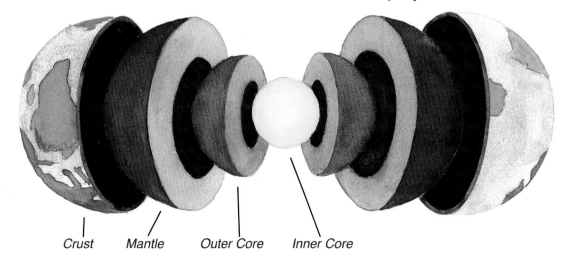

Crust   Mantle   Outer Core   Inner Core

Comets

Comets are often considered very beautiful, but they have a violent history. Comets are chunks of rock and ice. They have been described as "dirty snowballs."

As a comet orbits the sun, it comes close enough to be warmed by the sun's heat. Some of the ice begins to evaporate, and the vapor forms a lovely tail. The tail may be 100 million miles long.

Comets are chunks of rock and ice that develop a tail of vapor that has been evaporated by the sun.

When we see a comet, we are really seeing the sunlight reflected from its long tail.

The vapor in a comet's tail is lost to space forever. Every time a comet orbits close to the sun, it forms a new tail. After passing by the sun a number of times, a comet will have lost all of its ice, and can no longer form a tail. With no tail, the comet cannot be seen from earth. It is said to be a "burned-out" comet.

Astronomers believe that burned-out comets are no different from asteroids. This means that comets came from the same planetary explosion that formed the asteroids.

Since comets are burning out, the number of visible comets is declining. Really bright comets are rare now. The last appearance of Halley's comet, one of the most visible comets, was in 1986. Although millions of people looked forward to seeing Halley's Comet, it was actually hard to see even at night, yet brilliant comets were common in ancient times.

The Romans are said to have seen quite a few comets a year, some of them visible in broad daylight. Like other events associated with cosmic catastrophes, appearances of comets were more common and more intense in the past.

Earth

Halley's Comet

Orbit of Comet

The orbit of Halley's comet is so large that it passes by the earth once every 76 years or so.

The Age of Comets

How many trips can a comet make by the sun before it burns out? Dr. Fred Whipple, a world authority on comets, has estimated about 200. Then the comet would be invisible from earth. Considering Halley's comet orbit of 76 years as average,

As comets travel around the sun, they are slowly evaporated by its heat. It is estimated that a comet could make about 200 trips before it burned out. Comets must be less than 15,000 years old.

this means that comets must be less than 15,000 years old or so. This is much less than the presumed evolutionary age of 5 billion years, and is a serious problem for astronomers who believe in evolution.

To get around this problem, some astronomers have claimed that there is a huge sphere of rock and ice surrounding the solar system way out beyond Pluto. This sphere is called the Oort Cloud after the Dutch astronomer who first thought of it.

According to this idea, every now and then some fragments of rock and ice leave the Oort Cloud to enter the inner solar system as comets. With the Oort Cloud continuously supplying new comets, the solar system can be very old though individual comets do not last very long.

There are two problems with the Oort Cloud: (1) no astronomer has ever observed it, though there have been several efforts to detect it with space probes; and (2) historical evidence shows that people saw comets more often in ancient times, which means that the number of comets really is declining without being replenished.

Meteor Showers

When a meteor enters the earth's atmosphere, it gets extremely hot and glows with heat from atmospheric friction. Most meteors are the size of pebbles or dust grains and burn up in a few seconds or less.

As a meteor burns, it produces a streak of light called a "shooting star." A shooting star is not a star at all in the modern sense. Until a few centuries ago, however, a "star" was considered to be any heavenly object besides the sun or the moon, and the term "shooting star" reflects that old usage.

Like comets, meteors seem to be asteroids that have escaped from the asteroid belt, but without the ice which would evaporate to produce a visible tail when they come close to the sun. There are several swarms of meteors, sometimes called "meteor showers," that regularly cross the earth's orbit. Some of these meteor swarms are known from eyewitness accounts to be pieces of comets that disintegrated.

One of the most dependable and noticeable meteor showers is the Perseids, visible for 2 or 3 weeks around mid-August. You may be able to count up to 100 meteor trails a minute when a meteor shower is at its peak.

Occasionally meteors the size of huge boulders pass within a few miles of the ground. The death-dealing potential of such meteors shows that, like comets, meteors were not part of God's originally perfect, life-supporting creation. In the past, some of these huge meteors have actually landed.

A meteor shower occurs when meteors burn up in the earth's atmosphere, such as this fireball from the Leonid meteor shower.

James W. Young - 1966

Big Meteor Craters

One of the largest meteor impact craters on earth is the Arizona Meteor Crater near Winslow, Arizona. It is about 600 feet deep and one mile across. Catastrophes like the impact that formed this crater are not happening today. As with other cosmic catastrophes, the level of destruction was higher in the past.

In Canada, for instance, there is the Chubb Meteor Crater with a diameter of about two miles. Now a lake, it was not recognized as a crater until aerial photography showed its circular outline. Later research confirmed that it was made by a huge meteor.

Even the huge Chubb crater is dwarfed by the Sudbury meteor deposits, also in Canada. Meteors are often rich in iron and nickel, and the nickel-rich veins at Sudbury provide 20 percent of the world supply of nickel. This means that there is a good chance that the nickel in coinage is actually from outer space. The nickel in your pocket change may be partly extraterrestrial!

This meteor crater in Arizona is one of the largest in the world, measuring 600 feet deep and a mile across.

Did an Asteroid or Meteor Kill the Dinosaurs?

Could massive impacts have caused dinosaur extinctions and other death on a global scale? According to this idea, the dinosaurs did not die directly from any impacts, but from climate changes caused by the impacts. The impacts would have thrown tremendous amounts of dust and debris into the atmosphere, where it would have prevented sunlight from reaching the plants the dinosaurs ate. Most vegetation died and the dinosaurs starved. Is this story true?

Asteroid impacts massive enough to kill all the dinosaurs should have left some traces of meteors in the fossil-bearing rocks. Yet the rocks in which fossils are found contain no certain fragments of meteors.

Neither is there any crater big enough to match such an impact. All known impact craters are too small to have come from meteors big enough to cause global extinctions. In spite of this, some scientists have claimed that they have found tremendously large impact craters, such as the Chicxulub (chick-SHOE-lubb) Crater in Mexico.

However, the Chicxulub Crater is not a new discovery. It has been known for decades, and was said to be caused by a volcano before it was popular to account for dinosaur extinction by meteor impacts. Even though past meteor impacts probably killed many people and animals here and there, worldwide extinctions are best explained by climate changes following the flood.

Furthermore, in spite of the current interest in future asteroid impacts, there is absolutely no scientific evidence that big impacts will occur in the future.

There is little evidence that an asteroid killed the dinosaurs. Worldwide extinctions are best explained by climate changes after the flood.

Big Meteorites

When a meteor lands on earth it is called a meteorite. The largest known meteorite is the 66-ton Hoba meteorite in Namibia, South Africa. It left no crater, apparently because it did not make a direct hit on the earth's surface, but entered at a glancing angle. It is so large that no one has tried to move it to a museum.

Perhaps the most catastrophic impact event of modern times was the so-called "Tunguska event" in Siberia in 1908. There was an explosion heard 70 miles away, and it flattened 770 square miles of forest. No crater was formed and no one was hurt, but the Soviets claimed that they found meteorite fragments at the site. Apparently the meteorite exploded before it hit the ground.

On the other hand, some astronomers believe that the Tunguska event may have been due to a comet colliding with the earth. Since comets are similar to meteors, scientists have not been able to rule out either one of these possibilities.

Some meteorites have survived their fall to the earth. The Ahnighito Meteorite, in the American Museum of Natural History, is the largest known meteorite in North America and weighs over 36 tons.

People Have Seen Big Meteors Land

Twice in two decades small meteors struck the same town of Wethersfield, Connecticut — once in 1971 and again in 1982. In 1954 a meteor several inches across tore through the ceiling of a house in Syllacauga, Alabama. After ripping through the ceiling, the meteor nicked the radio in the living room, struck the lady of the house as she was napping on the sofa, then bounced off the sofa onto the floor. No one was killed in these events, nor have there been any recorded deaths in other similar events in modern times.

This is in contrast to the possibly high death toll from massive ancient impacts. Could the tremendously destructive meteor impacts of the ancient past be the cause of the fear of comets and meteors which was so common in ancient times?

The same cultures which were so afraid of meteors and comets actually worshiped most of the other heavenly bodies, rather than being afraid of them. Why the ancient fear of comets and meteors, unless there was some basis in past experience?[8]

The Bible tells us that man was created in the image of God. This means that even the earliest peoples were rational. They had genuine reasons for their fears of unpredictable cosmic events.

As time passed, people lost their fear of meteors and comets. The memory of ancient catastrophes was forgotten. By the 1600s, when Edmund Halley (the namesake of Halley's comet) first explained the behavior of comets by Isaac Newton's laws of motion and gravitation, comets were no longer perceived as a threat to life, and people readily accepted Halley's ideas. Nevertheless, sin had left its mark on the cosmos, in the remnants of past violence which are so much a part of astronomy today.

This meteor fragment landed in western Australia in 1960. It is believed to be from the asteroid Vesta and is made almost entirely of the mineral pyroxene, common in lava flows (shown actual size).

Chapter 11

ARE THERE OTHER PLANETS IN OTHER SOLAR SYSTEMS?

Astronomers have found no planets outside our solar system. Furthermore, scientists do not know of any planets around any stars except the sun. As far as science can determine, our solar system is absolutely unique.

Some scientists who believe in evolution are not satisfied with this conclusion. To them, life should be evolving in many places in the universe. They believe there should be other solar systems with planets having life on them.

Sometimes this desire to find other planets and solar systems leads to misleading newspaper and magazine headlines. *Sky and Telescope*, for instance, published an issue with the cover story, "New Planets Discovered!"[9] *Astronomy* magazine published an article entitled, "Two New Solar Systems."[10] Titles like these give the impression that astronomers have made new planetary discoveries.

The question we must ask when we see such headlines is, what did the astronomers really observe? It is impossible for astronomers to see planets outside our solar system directly, even with the most sophisticated telescopes. Because planets shine only by reflected light, any such planets would be far too dim to see. Stars and galaxies are the only directly observable objects outside our solar system.

"Hubble's First Direct Look At Possible Planet Around Another Star" is the headline from this photo taken on August 4, 1997. The bright light in the middle is two binary stars orbiting each other and the faint object in the bottom left is the "possible" new planet. With every new planet story having been found false, even the headline suggests that astronomers are only guessing.

Why Do Some Astronomers Believe There Are Other Solar Systems?

Claims of new planets do not come from actually observing any planets. These claims are based on observing stars with certain characteristics. Some astronomers assume that these characteristics are signs of new planets.

Most stars, for example, are members of multiple star systems in which most of the stars are not easily visible because they are dim. Alpha Centauri used to be thought of as a single star. Then astronomers discovered that Alpha Centauri has a companion star, making a "double" or "binary" star system. Eventually, astronomers discovered another star in the Alpha Centauri system. Now we know that this system has at least three stars, but two of them are extremely dim.

In another system such as Sirius A and Sirius B, the gravitational force of the dimmer star tugs on the brighter one, making it "wobble." The stellar companion of Sirius A was suspected to exist long before it could be seen, because astronomers could see the wobbling motion of Sirius A. Telescopes powerful enough to see the suspected companion were not developed until years later. Astronomers have now carefully studied such dim companions and have found them to be stars, not planets.

Since most stars are in multiple systems, most stars wobble, being pulled by unseen stars too dim to observe. If the dim companions are especially hard to observe, astronomers sometimes assume that they must be planets in a kind of solar system. This was the case in the *Sky and Telescope* and *Astronomy* articles mentioned earlier. Both of these articles acknowledged that the alleged planets might be dim stars. *Sky and Telescope* has even acknowledged that all previous claims of new planets have been "debunked," including the earlier "New Planets Discovered!" headline.[11]

A second common property of stars is that they are surrounded by clouds of gas. Most stars are quite unstable and throw off gases explosively from time to time. Evolutionists sometimes think of such a gas cloud as evidence of a solar system in formation. According to this idea, our own solar system evolved over billions of years from a cloud of gas, so why should the same thing not be happening elsewhere?

Of course, our solar system did not evolve at all, and what's more, laboratory tests have confirmed that it's impossible for small particles of debris somehow to stick together and begin forming a planet. The real meaning of the debris surrounding so many stars is that the cosmos is self-destructing. It is dying, because it is all "groaning" under the curse of sin (Rom. 8:20–22).

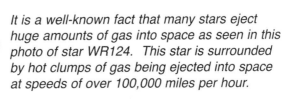

It is a well-known fact that many stars eject huge amounts of gas into space as seen in this photo of star WR124. This star is surrounded by hot clumps of gas being ejected into space at speeds of over 100,000 miles per hour.

Binary Stars

These photos of the Kruger 60 binary star system show the rotation of a smaller star around the larger one (upper right of each photo). These stars have an orbital period of 44.5 years. Multiple star systems are often mistaken for new "solar systems," with the smaller stars being confused with "planets."

Is There Extraterrestrial Life?

Extraterrestrial life (ET life, for short) is life which supposedly lives somewhere besides the earth. Some astronomers have proposed that strange forms of life might

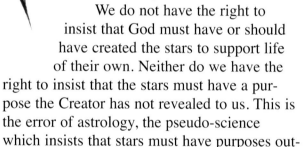

There is no evidence of extraterrestrial life in the universe.

exist on other moons, such as Io and Europa (moons of Jupiter), or Saturn's moon, Titan. However, there is absolutely no evidence of any life on these moons. Astronomers have found no evidence of ET life anywhere.[12]

Nevertheless, some scientists have coined the term "exobiology," meaning the study of extraterrestrial life. Theodosius Dobzhansky, the late evolutionist known worldwide in academic circles, has noted that exobiology is the only scientific discipline whose "subject matter has never been observed and may not exist."[13]

The search for ET life has been officially designated by NASA as the "Search for Extraterrestrial Intelligence," or SETI. The Bible, however, makes no mention of any life living off the earth except God and the angels. This is significant, because the Bible was not written to apply only to the earth. The Bible in Genesis chapter 1 makes sweeping statements of purpose which are true for all places in the cosmos (Gen. 1:14–18).

We do not have the right to insist that God must have or should have created the stars to support life of their own. Neither do we have the right to insist that the stars must have a purpose the Creator has not revealed to us. This is the error of astrology, the pseudo-science which insists that stars must have purposes outside the ones revealed by the Creator.

What Is Life?

Hebrews 4:15 tells us about genuine "ET life," our Creator God who is the author of all life. This verse tells us that He is not a fearful alien. He can "be touched with the feeling of our infirmities." We are not alone.

Many scientists have realized that the Search for Extraterrestrial Intelligence is really a search for spiritual intelligence.[14] Instead of searching for extraterrestrial intelligence, each of us must find spiritual life in the Lord Jesus Christ.

Each of us must trust Him alone for personal salvation. Those who have trusted Christ alone can anticipate an eternity with Him, a future far more wonderful than the most imaginative science fiction.

What Are UFOs?

UFO stands for "unidentified flying object." Most UFOs are nothing mysterious at all. Many UFO sightings turn out to be clouds, ordinary planes, weather balloons, or artificial satellites high in the sky which have been misidentified as something strange.

Of the small remaining number of UFO sightings, most of them probably involve military technology not yet made known to the public. Flight tests of this technology seem strange and unfamiliar to anyone who happens to see it from a distance.

Finally, there is the possibility of demonic influence in some UFO phenomena. How can we put this possibility in perspective?

Astronomy has been an especially fertile ground for satanic deception. Cosmic evolution and astrology trap many people in systems of belief which prevent them from ever coming to Christ for salvation. An obsession with UFOs is simply one more possible trap.

Satan uses the search for aliens and UFOs as a deception to keep many people from finding the true source of salvation. Through Jesus Christ and His Word we can find eternal salvation and wisdom for this life without having to search elsewhere for a higher intelligence.

For many people, the widespread belief in extraterrestrial intelligence and UFO intelligence may be another way of avoiding their personal accountability to God. The so-called "Roswell incident" of 1947, in which extraterrestrial beings allegedly landed near Roswell, New Mexico, has become an obsession for perhaps millions of people.

Whatever happened at Roswell, the Roswell incident has convinced many people that wisdom and intelligence are to be found somewhere out in space. Satan, the god of this world, is pleased to use any tactic that will keep a person from looking to the God of creation for true salvation and intelligence.

Yet, the Bible tells us that those who have come to Jesus Christ alone for personal salvation can have wisdom and intelligence simply by asking Him for it (James 1:5). Why should we search anywhere else?

Endnotes

1. J.B. Russell, *Inventing the Flat Earth* (New York: Praeger, 1991), p. ix–x.

2. A. Montgomery and L. Dolphin, "Is the Velocity of Light Constant in Time?" *Galilean Electrodynamics*, May/June 1993, p. 1.

3. M.M. Waldrop, "Why Do Planets Have Rings?" *Science 83*, vol. 4, March 1983, p. 112.

4. W.K. Hartmann, *Astronomy* (Belmont, CA: Wadsworth Publishing, 1991), p. 255.

5. W.R. Corliss, *Mysterious Universe: A Handbook of Astronomical Anomalies* (Glen Arm, MD: The Sourcebook Project, 1979), p. 534.

6. Ibid., p. 227.

7. R.V. Gentry, *Creation's Tiny Mystery* (Knoxville, TN: Earth Science Associates, 1992).

8. W.K. Hartmann, *Astronomy* (Belmont, CA: Wadsworth Publishing, 1991), p. 273.

9. R.T. Feinberg, "Pulsars, Planets, and Pathos," *Sky and Telescope*, vol. 88, May 1992, p. 493 and cover.

10. R. Naeye, "Two New Solar Systems," *Astronomy*, vol. 24, April 1996, p. 50.

11. A.M. MacRobert and J. Rother, "The Planet of 51 Pegasi," *Sky and Telescope*, vol. 91, January 1995, p. 38.

12. T.P. Snow, *Essentials of the Dynamic Universe* (St. Paul, MN: West Publishing, 1987), p. 485.

13. T. Dobzhansky et al., *Evolution* (San Francisco, CA: W.H. Freeman, 1977), p. 366.

14. J.F. Baugher, *On Civilized Stars* (Englewood Cliffs, NJ: Prentice-Hall, 1985), p. x–xi.

    D. Overbye, "Is Anyone Out There?" *Discover*, vol. 3, March 1982, p. 22.

    T.P. Snow, *Essentials of the Dynamic Universe* (St. Paul, MN: West Publishing, 1987), p. 499.

Illustration/ Photo Credits

A=All, T=Top, M=Middle, B=Bottom, L=Left, R=Right

Antique Maps CD: 25T

Astronomy and Space CD: 5, 6, 7A, 12T, 12B, 13TL, 13TR, 13BL, 14, 15T, 16, 17, 19B, 20T, 21B, 26BL, 33B, 36A, 37A, 38T, 38B, 40A, 41A, 42TR, 44TR, 44BL, 47BL, 47BR, 50, 54T, 54M, 55B, 56, 57A, 59, 60A, 67A

Institute for Creation Research: 22M, 22BR, 24BL, 27A, 51A, 65T

National Space Science Data Center: 26TR, 52B, 72, 73A

Bryan Miller: 8, 10A, 11A, 12M, 13BR, 15B, 18, 19T, 20M, 21T, 22BL, 23A, 24T, 28B, 38M, 42M, 42B, 43B, 44M, 49T, 49ML, 49BR, 52T, 53, 55T, 62M, 63BL, 66, 68, 71T, 74, 75

NASA: 1, 28T, 29A, 30A, 31, 32A, 33T, 34T, 35BL, 39T, 39BR, 44BR, 45A, 46A, 47TL, 47 TR, 48A, 49M, 54B, 58, 61A, 62T, 63TL, 63TR, 63MR, 64A, 65B, 69A, 71B

New Leaf Press: 24BR, 70

Glossary

Asteroids —chunks of rock and dust located mainly between Mars and Jupiter

Astrology — the false belief that the stars direct our lives

Astronomy — the scientific study of the sun, moons, planets and stars

Big Bang — the false belief that the universe began with a cosmic explosion

Celestial bodies —objects in the heavens; the sun, moons, planets and stars

Constellations — patterns of stars in the sky

Corona — outer layer of gases surrounding the sun, normally visible only during a total solar eclipse

Cosmic evolution —the false belief that the universe developed without being created

Eclipse —the blocking of one object's light by another; for example, a solar eclipse, in which the moon blocks the sun's light

Galaxy clusters — groups of galaxies

Galaxies — huge groups of stars containing about 100 billion stars apiece

Light-year — the distance light travels in one year, about 6 trillion miles

Look-back time —the time before the present when light left the stars and galaxies we see

Lunar recession — the slow motion of the moon away from the earth

Meteorite — a meteor which has landed on earth

Milky Way — the galaxy in which the earth is located

Nebular hypothesis — the false belief that the solar system evolved from a cloud of gas

Neutrinos — small particles thought to be produced by nuclear fusion in the sun

Parallax — the apparent motion of nearby objects when we travel, compared with distant objects which seem not to move at all

Prograde rotation — the normal planetary rotation in which the sun rises in the east and sets in the west

Retrograde rotation — opposite of prograde; the sun rises in the west and sets in the east

SETI — the Search for Extraterrestrial Intelligence

Spectrum — the rainbow of colors made by a prism splitting light into its separate parts

Supernova remnant — the debris left over from the explosion of a star

UFOs — Unidentified Flying Objects

Variable star — a star whose output of light and energy changes drastically over a period of time

Index

A

Asteroids, 62, 63
    Ceres, 62
    Gaspra, 62
Astronomy, as a revelation of God, 5
    definition of, 6

B

Babel, Tower of, 24, 25
Bible, references to the
    Genesis 1:1, 14
    Genesis 1:5, 40
    Genesis 1:13, 40

Genesis 1:14-18, 23, 24, 37, 58, 74
Genesis 1:16, 22, 38, 50
Genesis 1:19, 38, 40
Genesis 1:31, 16, 58
Genesis 2:1, 17
Genesis 3:17
Genesis 8:1, 61
Genesis 10-11, 24
Genesis 11:15, 25
Psalm 19:1, 5
Psalm 33:6, 14
Psalm 143:8, 6
Isaiah 40:22, 20

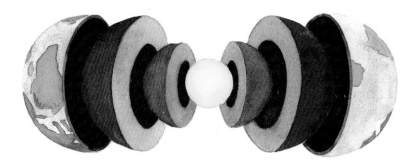

Isaiah 45:16, 61
Jeremiah 31:37, 10
Romans 6:20-22, 73
Romans 8:22, 56
James 1:5, 75
James 4:13-15, 6
Hebrews 1:11, 53
Hebrews 4:15, 74
Big Bang, 16
Big Dipper, 26
Black holes, 53

C

Calendars, lunar, 23
    solar, 23
Comets, 67, 68
    age of, 68
    Halley, 67
Constellations, 26, 27
    Orion, 25
    Serpens, 25
    Ursa Major, 25'
Cosmic catastrophes, 56, 61-66
Creation, 17, 61
    age of, 55
    by God's word alone, 14
    importance of the biblical record, 17
    not an evolutionary process, 14
    of moons, 15
    of the moon, 38
    of planets, 15, 22, 44, 48, 49
    purpose of, 37
    of stars, 22, 50
    of the universe, 14

DEF

Dinosaur extinction, 70
Earth, purpose, 36
    uniqueness, 36
Eclipses, lunar, 20
    solar, 21
Flood, the, 61, 70

G

Galaxies
    Andromeda, 8, 54
    Milky Way, 12
    number of, 7

Very Large Magellanic Cloud, 54
Galaxy clusters, 7
Greenwich Mean Time, 24

H

Helmholtz, Hermann von, 42
Hipparchus, 52
Hubble Space Telescope, 49

LM

Look-back time, 35
Meteors, 68, 69, 70
Meteor craters, 69
Meteorites, 70, 71
Meteor showers, 68, 69
    shooting stars, 68
Moon, the, 8, 15, 18
    age, 39
    distance from the earth, 8
    lunar landings, 28
    origin, 38
    phases, 18
Moons of planets, 46, 47
    Callisto, 46
    Charon, 49
    Deimos, 63
    Europa, 46
    Ganymede, 46
    Io, 46
    Miranda, 61
    Phobos, 63
    Titan, 47

N

Nebular hypothesis, 43, 44
Neutrinos, 42

PR

Parallax, 11
Planets, 15
    Earth, 12
    Jupiter, 12, 13, 37, 37, 47, 66
    Mars, 12, 13, 32, 45, 64, 65
        Mars rocks, 45
        Martian flood, 65
        no life on, 45
    Mercury, 12, 32, 44, 66
    Neptune, 12, 33, 49, 66

Pluto, 12, 13, 37, 49
    purpose of, 37
    Saturn, 12, 13, 33, 48, 66
        age, 60
    Uranus, 12, 33, 48, 66
    Venus, 8, 32, 44, 66
Prograde rotation, 44
Retrograde rotation, 44
Rings of planets
    Jupiter, 60
    Saturn, 47
    Uranus, 48
Rockets, 28, 29

S

Space missions, 28, 29, 30
    Apollo 8, 29
    Apollo 11, 30
    Apollo 13, 35
    Galileo, 35
    Rover, 27, 45
    Viking, 37
Space Shuttle, 31, 33
Space stations, 31
    Mir, 31, 32
Star birth, myth of, 59
Star death, 56
    of the sun, 57
Star names, 26, 27
Stars, alpha-Centauri, 8
    beta-Pictoris, 59
    Betelgeuse, 26, 52, 59
    distances, 11
    elements in, 51
    magnitudes, 52
    North Star (Polaris), 22
    number of, 50
    Proxima Centauri, 8, 9
    spectral classes, 51

Star systems, 40, 73
    binary, 73
    double, 73
Sun, the, 13
    age, 43
    corona, 19
    nuclear fusion in, 42
    purpose, 40
    shrinkage of, 42, 43
    sunspots, 19
    uniqueness, 40, 41
Supernova remnants, 57
Crab Nebula, 57, 58
Ring Nebula, 56

TUV

Telescopes, reflector, 20, 21
    refractor, 20
Total eclipses, 19
Universe, age, 53
    edge of, 53
    expansion of, 17
    origin, 15
    other universes, 10
    size of, 8, 12
Variable stars, 41, 73
von Braun, Werner, 34

The sun is 1,000 times larger than Jupiter and 1 million times larger than Earth. It is almost 1 million miles across! Its surface is about 10,000°F.

Mercury

> Biggest planet: Jupiter (1,000 times larger than Earth)
> Smallest planet: Pluto (200 times smaller than Earth)
> Longest day: Venus (rotates once every 243 Earth days)
> Shortest day: Jupiter (rotates once every 10 hours)
> Longest year: Pluto (248 Earth years)
> Shortest year: Mercury (88 Earth days)

ion

Ve...

Earth

Mars

Jupiter

...aturn

...noon on July 20, 1969. The first man on
...ng, followed by Edwin "Buzz" Aldrin.

...oring God's Creat...

The first space shuttle, Columbia, launched on April 12, 1981.

The first man landed on the ... the moon was Neil Arms...

> Closest to the sun: Mercury
> Farthest from the sun: Pluto
> Hottest surface: Venus (900°F)
> Coldest surface: Pluto (-400°F)

Uranus

Neptune

Pluto